The Type A's Guide to Mindfulness

Meditation for Busy Minds and Busy People

Melissa Eisler
www.mindfulminutes.com

The Type A's Guide to Mindfulness:
Meditation for Busy Minds and Busy People

Copyright © 2015 by Melissa Eisler

Publisher: Mindful Minutes

All rights reserved. No part of this publication may be reproduced, distributed, transmitted or copied in any form or by any means, including photocopying, recording, or other electronic or mechanical methods, without the prior written permission from the publisher, except for the use of brief quotations in a book review and certain other noncommercial uses permitted by copyright law. For permission requests, write to the publisher at
Melissa@MindfulMinutes.com.

Disclaimers

No Medical Advice
The information provided in this book reflects the opinion of the author and is to be used for instructional and entertainment purposes only. The recommendations made are not intended to diagnose or prescribe for medical or psychological conditions, or to replace the relationship of a qualified healthcare provider. It is strictly meant to be the sharing of information from the research and experience of the author. It is sold with the understanding that the publisher and author are not engaged in rendering psychological, health, legal, financial, career, or other professional services. If expert assistance or counseling is needed, the services of a professional should be sought. The author is not a lawyer, doctor, or mental health professional, so please use your best judgment always when applying the information from this book into your own life.

Third Party Disclaimer
The third party companies, websites, and people mentioned in this book are included solely as a convenience to you. The author is not to be held responsible for any information given from third parties mentioned in the book.

With Gratitude

An abundant amount of gratitude goes to my teachers, students, friends, and family who have supported me over the years, taught me important life lessons, and given me advice and motivation. Special thanks to:

My brother, Dave—who is always willing to give me legal advice in exchange for green smoothies.
Michael Clarke—who guided and motivated me through the crazy world of e-publishing.
Karson and Mitch McGinley—who are the most supportive and inspiring studio owners a girl could ever hope to work for.
Teresa Austin—who mentored me in my early years of teaching and introduced me to the rewarding world of teaching children.
Casey Jones—who's been my rock and best bud for the last couple of decades.
Katerina Suchkova—who pushed me forward when I needed it most and helped me build Mindful Minutes.
Sam Watts—who gently encouraged me to be more vulnerable.
My grandmother, Lillian Richman—who always listens, has my back, and is genuinely interested in talking about mindfulness at the young age of 92.
My mother—who instilled the workaholic in me, and years later, taught me to slow down.
My father—who passed along his creative genes and will forever remain my biggest role model.
And Angela Carlon—who piqued my interest in meditation a dozen years ago.

Your Free Gift!

As a thank you for buying my book, I've created a free audio file for a guided meditation. The guided meditation is only ten minutes and is sure to help you settle your mind and ease stress.

To receive your free gift, go to:

http://mindfulminutes.com/Book-Guided-Meditation-Gift

Table of Contents

Introduction: Letter from the Author 1

Chapter 1: What Is Meditation—and What Is it NOT? 13

Chapter 2: Oh, the Many Ways to Practice Mindfulness ... 45

Chapter 3: Ten Benefits of Meditation That'll Really Help Type As 71

Chapter 4: How to Meditate—Steps to Get You Started .. 81

Chapter 5: How to Squeeze in a Meditation Anytime, Anywhere 101

Chapter 6: The Role of the Breath in Mindfulness 113

Chapter 7: Ten Common Obstacles for New Meditators and How to Overcome Them 125

Chapter 8: Ten Short Meditations and Mindfulness Exercises for When You're Way Too Busy 147

Final Note from the Author 189

References 193

About the Author 201

Introduction:
Letter from the Author

Thank you so much for reading my book, *The Type A's Guide to Mindfulness: Meditation for Busy Minds and Busy People*. This book will give you an overview of the power of mindfulness and teach you some practical tools so you can start practicing *now* . . . even if you think you don't have time.

You're probably reading this because you have a busy life. So why should you spend your precious time meditating? Why is it the most important thing you can do for yourself right now?

Mindfulness practices—like meditation, mindful breathing, and yoga—have helped me cope with stress and anxiety, gain perspective, be more productive, and overall live a more balanced and healthy life. They've gotten me through 10 years in the corporate world, through the loss of loved ones, breakups, injuries, and have taught me how to manage the stress that used to overwhelm me. It's my hope that the practices, stories, and information I share will help you, too.

When I first started on the path of learning about mindfulness and meditation, I was in search of that one big thing I needed to learn, accomplish or practice in order to move past my challenges. But what I found (through a lot of mistakes and lessons along the way) was that there's not just *one* thing—there are a lot of little things. This book is a compilation of the many lessons and practices I've learned that have helped me over the years.

You've probably heard a lot of buzz about meditation and mindfulness. It's exploded in the media. I'm grateful for this, because when *Time* magazine publishes a cover piece like "The Mindful Revolution," or *60-Minutes'* Anderson Cooper explores mindfulness at a weekend retreat and broadcasts it to mainstream audiences, it brings awareness to practices that have helped me so much in my life.

So, whether you heard about it from the media, a friend, family member, co-worker, or your doctor—even if you already have a meditation practice but are having a hard time squeezing it into your busy schedule—I wrote this book to show you how you can fit meditation and mindfulness into your busy, modern—sometimes chaotic—lifestyle.

In this book, you'll find:

- A multi-response answer to "why should I spend my precious, limited time meditating?" complete with scientific research, personal examples, and experiential reasons that will get you excited to start your practice
- Practical meditation and mindfulness techniques
- Awareness and relaxation exercises to help you manage your stress
- A step-by-step guide on how to start a meditation or mindfulness practice
- Tips for how to overcome common obstacles in meditation (*trust me, I've been there*)
- How to fit meditation into your day using whatever time is available to you

Since we'll be spending some time together, I want to tell you a little about who I am and why I'm qualified to teach you about mindfulness. Here we go . . .

My Story

I've spent my entire life identifying closely with being busy—as someone who has always been enthusiastic about life and people and all of the opportunities that are constantly unfolding. I'm a certified yoga instructor (E-RYT-200), certified Primordial Sound Meditation instructor, as well as a content strategist, writer and editor.

Currently, my full-time job is with the Chopra Center for Wellbeing, Deepak Chopra's mind-body wellness center, where I'm the senior content strategist. On the side, I freelance as a copywriter and content strategist.

I also teach Vinyasa yoga classes to a wonderful community of dedicated yogis at my favorite studio in San Diego; I teach meditation, guided breathwork and yoga to kids and families in the oncology ward at Rady's Children's Hospital; and I teach worker-bees in the corporate world. It's a fun challenge for me to find the right way to explain mindfulness to such different types of people.

I'd like to rewind for a moment and share a little about the roots of my Type A personality and anxiety. Since they both showed up in my life at an early age, I'll start there and walk you through how they played their roles—and played into one another—throughout my life.

I developed my Type A nature growing up on the east coast; my parents were both New Yorkers and I grew up with the mantras "work, work, work" and "achieve, achieve, achieve." Grades were very important, and failure was feared. My mom was a workaholic when I was young, and she worked herself into a very serious illness by the time she was 40. I was eight at the time, and I developed anxiety.

I still remember feeling totally consumed with worry, of course about my mom's surgeries and disease—*What would happen if she could no longer take care of me?* But I also worried about what would happen if I fell off stage during the school play—*Would everybody laugh at me?* And what if my best friend, Adrienne, got mad at me—*Would she stop coming over to play?* And how about if I said the wrong answer in front of my whole third grade class—*Would anyone still talk to me?*

I had frequent nightmares of a witch chasing me down a hill and she would often appear in my thoughts when I was trying to do my homework. I also swore there were monsters disguised as the stuffed puppies that sat perfectly on my bed... *I spent a lot of time in my head.*

I was also spending a lot of time in the hospital with my family (a very stressful environment), and because of the stress my family was dealing with, and the fact that I was doing well in school, my issues with anxiety went undiagnosed.

My high school days were spent developing the "skills" of distracting myself and keeping busy—this was relatively normal where I grew up. A true overachiever: I skipped lunch all four years to take an extra elective, was president of theater, photo editor of the yearbook, a member of

All-State Choir, an honors student, and took either dance or music lessons five days a week.

Fast forward to college and neither the stress in my environment, nor my anxiety, improved. I continued to mistakenly choose distraction as a way to handle the stress.

I didn't consider dealing with emotions, feelings, and anxieties to be part of my priority list. At age nineteen, I lost my father to cancer, which was a two-year battle. My father was the closest person in my life at the time and the rock of our family. Instead of acknowledging the loss, I moved forward like a motor. I was also the go-to caretaker for my mother, who was getting sicker; I didn't take the time to grieve or recognize the feelings of loss and anxiety that followed. And I certainly didn't realize that those feelings would only multiply if I didn't deal with them.

As these difficult life events unfolded, I took on more and more to distract and push myself. I most definitely kept my grades high, but I also added bartending, internships, studying abroad, and an honors thesis . . . I was getting panic attacks every day and I wouldn't slow down and sit with what was actually rising inside.

I would just be walking to class or at the gym and—all of a sudden—I would think my breathing had stopped. I would be brought to my knees or the closest couch and have to use all of my energy just to find my next breath. My mind would spin with worry and my body would freeze, until I gathered myself enough to push forward into the next self-declared important task. If anyone noticed or asked, I would pretend like I was totally fine. In true east coast fashion, I thought distraction was the solution.

I moved to California right after college and maintained my mantra of "work, work, work." I simultaneously held five jobs my first year while a host of other challenges and losses piled up. My anxiety was at its peak and I would've tried anything to help mollify that feeling. All I could do to settle my nerves was work out and run, which helped only to a degree.

A friend suggested I start doing yoga; she told me it would help with the anxiety. So I started going to class every Tuesday night at the gym. It would be an understatement to say that I didn't like it at first—it was way too slow for me. But I was told it would help my anxiety, so I'd show up to class every week. The part I disliked most about my early yoga classes was *Savasana*, which is the final resting pose in yoga where you're supposed to just chill. I didn't understand the point of lying down on a yoga mat in the middle of a stinky gym doing nothing. Every time class started winding down, I'd try to sneak out just before *Savasana*.

At the time, *Savasana*, meditation, and slower-paced yoga *highlighted* my anxiety to me. As soon as quiet or stillness came over my yoga mat, my mind would spiral out of control: *What on earth was I thinking when I moved to California by myself? I can't even find a good job here . . . Why can't I find a good job—is there something wrong with me? Maybe I should rework my resume . . . again. Or maybe I should put more effort into the stupid job I do have—I mean, why didn't I finish the assignment my boss gave me on Thursday? How can I be a better employee? More importantly, how can I be a better daughter, friend, and roommate? Why am I so scared of failing??* **If the practice was too slow, my mind totally took over and ruined the experience for me. I thought I couldn't help that; I thought quiet time just wasn't meant for Type As like me.**

After about six months into practicing yoga, I made a commitment to try to find a class I actually liked. I joined a studio and started with the level three Vinyasa class—which is, for those who aren't familiar, a very advanced class and I had no business being there. I didn't know anything about yoga and was completely unqualified to attend an advanced class, but I figured I would get a better workout at a level three class than a beginner's class. Sure enough, the fitness challenge kept me showing up consistently. And as I started practicing more, I noticed my anxiety levels go down, and my panic attacks stopped completely.

Little by little, I began settling into the power of what yoga really was. I even began taking *Savasana* seriously and exploring slower-paced classes and meditation.

At this time, I was working at a large company, putting in far beyond a full-time schedule as the director of a digital editorial team, managing writers, editors, and content strategy for multiple consumer platforms. For years, I would work all week in this corporate lifestyle, while diving into my yoga and meditation practice at night and on the weekends. Through corporate restructures, mergers, an IPO, eight bosses in eight years, plus all the different stresses that come with that life, my practice kept building. It helped me deal with the daily stress of corporate life and the pressures that came with leading a team.

I began my practice more than 10 years ago to get some exercise and deal with anxiety . . . but yoga was the bridge for me. It taught me to open and settle my mind and it slowly introduced me to mindfulness and meditation.

So, now you have some background on me and hopefully recognize that I've been in your shoes in one way or another. At the very least, I understand what it's like to have a full calendar and a serious career—yet I still find time for mindful moments and deep breaths, and you can too.

My Goal for This Book

My hope is that by writing this book, I can convince you of the possibilities and benefits of a consistent meditation practice, and inspire you to find some form of a mindfulness practice that works for you.

Whether your goal is to fight stress, find focus, manage pain or illness, gain clarity or direction, or all of the above—meditation is for you. I'm really excited to show you how it can easily integrate into your life . . . starting now.

After all, why put it off any longer? You have a much better, more balanced, and more fulfilling life just waiting for you once you're able to carve out some time to settle your mind.

Warmly,

Melissa Eisler

P.S. For more information, stories, meditations, and blogs about mindfulness, meditation, and life balance in the modern world, visit www.MindfulMinutes.com.

If you have any questions or comments as you're reading this book and getting started with your practice, please don't hesitate to reach out. The best place to reach me is on my Mindful Minutes Facebook: www.facebook.com/mindfulminutes; or on Twitter: @MelissaEisler. Or, if you have a story on how a mindfulness practice—or this book—helped you in your life, please share it with me. If you'd rather talk privately, feel free to send me a note at Melissa@MindfulMinutes.com.

I'd love to support you in your journey towards healthy, balanced, and mindful living.

Chapter 1:
What Is Meditation—and What Is it NOT?

"You can't stop the waves, but you can learn to surf."
~ Jon Kabat-Zinn

I didn't like the idea of meditation when I first heard about it, and I really didn't like the idea of meditation when I first experienced it. I didn't think meditation was for Type As, which—you'll come to learn over the course of this book—I most definitely am. And the idea of sitting still intimidated the hell out of me.

The truth is, I had the wrong idea about what meditation really is. I am a fast mover and a doer by nature and the thought of doing nothing totally freaked me out. The most used word in my vocabulary was busy, and I didn't jive with the notion of spending my precious time getting nothing done. There are very few things in life that intimidate me, but being unproductive, alone, and silent with my thoughts, used to be at the top of this list. At the same time, I'd heard the practice helped a lot of people, so I attempted to face the fear.

But when I finally got over the intimidation factor and tried meditation, I got nowhere and immediately thought I wasn't good at it. If you're Type A, you probably don't like failing at things, either. This only drove my neurosis further into a feverish cycle, making my self-critic the star of the show once again—and validating my theory that Type As couldn't meditate.

I spent years struggling with a practice, finding *really* good excuses why my meditation should wait until "tomorrow," and fumbling over the perfect time, the perfect meditation, the right style, an anxiety-ridden monkey mind, and everything in between. Shockingly, the reasons why I wanted to meditate in the first place (stress, anxiety, productivity) didn't improve when I kept putting it off.

At this point, no one had explained to me the process of meditation and what to expect. Or, maybe it had been explained but I hadn't been listening. I thought that having thoughts during meditation was proof that I wasn't born to be a meditator; I didn't realize that was just me being—a human being. I later learned that having thoughts while meditating is the most common experience that happens during meditation.

When I first tried to meditate, I had been suffering from a messy and long-standing case of anxiety, so slowing down only highlighted the anxiety for me. I hadn't given it a fair shot, and I hadn't learned in any formal setting. I was too intimidated, so I declared myself—and all Type As everywhere—unfit for meditation.

. . .That is, until I learned what meditation actually was, where it came from, what people are getting out of it, and how much I could benefit.

If meditation intimidates you in any way, know that I've been in that very place. The biggest thing I can say is that you don't have to be some sort of guru, yoga practitioner, lazy or calm person to meditate. You don't even have to be a particularly nice person to meditate. You just have to understand and accept that all humans have problems and all humans have thoughts. Meditation is not a way to erase your issues, challenges, or thoughts . . . it's simply a tool you can use anytime, anywhere to help you deal with life's challenges with greater ease.

What Is Meditation?

Meditation is a practice that leads to a state of thoughtful awareness. Any activity where you're consciously fostering a sense of deep awareness can be considered a form of meditation. Various meditation techniques work wonders to reduce stress and develop concentration, clarity, and calmer mental, physical, and emotional states.

Many people think of meditation as a religious or spiritual practice or a means of worship (more on meditation myths later). But really, meditation is just a means of interrupting our chaotic and constant thoughts—which all of us humans have and is now lovingly referred to as the monkey mind—with a dose of present moment awareness.

It's true that traditional meditation practices are done sitting down and that there are some styles and cultures that practice with prayer and intertwine with religious faith, but meditation has grown far beyond religious borders. It has become simply a way of life for many people across the world, across generations, and across faiths. It's now studied at universities, hospitals, and research labs around the world. In today's age, it's difficult for even the greatest skeptic to ignore the benefits of the practice.

Let's take a quick look at the background of meditation and how it's evolved into the mainstream practice it is today.

The Evolution of Meditation

Meditation has been around for thousands of years. But only in the last few has it been gaining mainstream momentum. If you look at the roots of the practice and where it started, it's taken a lot of credible voices to bring the practice into the global conversation. Here's a timeline of some of the key moments and highlights in meditation's history:

- **5,000-3,500 BCE:** No one knows the exact date of when meditation was born, but archaeologists and scholars agree that it has been around for approximately five thousand years.
- **1,500 BCE:** The earliest documented records on meditation were created in ancient India.
- **Between 600 and 500 BCE:** Meditation expanded in Taoist China and Buddhist India.
- **Between 400 BCE and 200 CE:** "The Bhagavad Gita" was written, an epic poem and scripture that explains the philosophy of yoga and meditation.
- **18th Century:** Fast Forward! It wasn't until the 18th century that the translations of the ancient teachings began to travel to the West.
- **1922**: The famous *Siddhartha* was written by Hermann Hesse, which discusses the story of Buddha's spiritual journey. There's nothing like a beautifully written book to bring a topic to mainstream awareness.
- **1950s**: The Vipassana movement—or insight meditation—developed in Burma.
- **1958**: Jack Kerouac published *The Dharma Bums*, discussing his early experience with Buddhism, successfully generating popular interest and curiosity to the practice of meditation.
- **1960s**: Hatha Yoga and Transcendental Meditation began to gain popularity in the United States and Europe.

- **1979**: Dr. Jon Kabat-Zinn founded Mindfulness Based Stress Reduction (MBSR), a program that launched at the University of Massachusetts to treat patients with chronic illnesses, which generated interest of mindfulness practices in the medical world.
- **1980s**: Meditation was still uncommon, and most people would probably think you were weird if you meditated. There were no mindfulness journal publications published in the 1980s. And certainly no magazines or newspapers thought mindfulness was worth covering.
- **1990**: Eight journal publications on mindfulness research were published.
- **1997**: Eckhart Tolle published *The Power of Now: A Guide to Spiritual Enlightenment* to introduce readers to the concept of present-moment awareness.
- **2000**: Twenty-two journal publications on mindfulness research were published, a moderate boost from eight a decade prior.
- **2004**: A study at the University of California, San Francisco concluded that there are strong links between chronic stress and poor health, which generated widespread press and launched more conversation and studies about meditation as a means to improve health.
- **2005**: Seventy journal publications on mindfulness research were published.
- **2005-2011**: A series of studies done at Harvard found that meditation changes the structure of

the brain—growing key areas of the brain linked with self-awareness, memory, learning, emotion-regulation and compassion while shrinking grey matter of the brain in the areas associated with stress. Google the study's senior author, Sara Lazar, to watch the TedX talk where she explains the research.

- **2007**: A study was published by the National Center for Complementary and Alternative Medicine, boasting that 9.4 percent of Americans have meditated.
- **2010**: Three hundred fifty-one journal publications on mindfulness research were published.
- **2013**: Deepak Chopra and Oprah Winfrey partner to bring a free 21-Day Meditation Experience program to the masses.
- **2014**: *Time* magazine published "The Mindful Revolution" on its cover in January 2014, shining a spotlight on meditation and its benefits.
- **2014**: Five hundred thirty-five journal publications on mindfulness research were published.

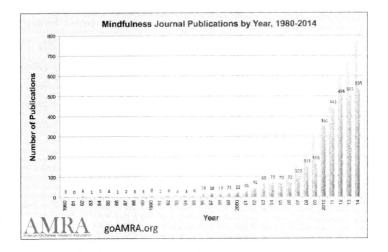

Figure Credit: illustrates the radical uptick in meditation research over the last 25 years.

What Is Mindfulness and Why Is it So Hard to Be Mindful?

"In case you haven't noticed, you have a mental dialogue going on inside your head that never stops. It just keeps going and going..."
~Michael Singer

Mindfulness is awareness of the present moment without judgment. There are stressful things that happen all the time. It is our *reaction* to those external events that often cause the larger dose of stress. Being mindful is the act of getting curious and observing what is happening, instead of reacting to it. During meditation, we are training our minds to be less reactive and more present with all things that grace our path.

The Monkey Mind Hard at Work

As humans, we have at least 50,000 thoughts every day, which means we have a thought approximately every 1.2 seconds. This human condition is often referred to as the *monkey mind*, and it can make us feel like we're crazy.

Buddhists gave our minds this nickname and defined it as "unsettled; restless; capricious; whimsical; fanciful; inconstant; confused; indecisive; uncontrollable." While not a particularly flattering nickname for our mind, it's quite accurate as our minds jump from thought to thought, just as a monkey leaps from tree to tree in search of the next banana.

The state of our mind is the driving force of our world. The mind controls how we move, it controls our energy levels, how we feel, and how we show up in the world. When our mind is operating in monkey mind mode we are not able to settle enough to focus, to get clear, or to take appropriate action in our lives.

Have you ever felt like there is something in your way of reaching a goal? Some roadblock or thing holding you back from taking a step forward? Sometimes it can be difficult to identify what that obstacle is, and many times it's ourselves—our own minds presenting us with limitations and distractions and insecurities and unhelpful thoughts. All of these things get in our way of achieving this, or completing that: finding the perfect job, getting a promotion, or simply getting in the way of us being right here, right now . . . in this present moment.

This state of our mind—*the monkey mind*—is part of being human. It's important to fully understand that all humans have had this same experience. We all suffer from the constant chatter of our minds—the voice inside our heads—and its innate nature to get lost in cycles and bounce, bop, and flop around. Left to its own agenda, the mind will be restless, unsettled, and often confused and uncontrollable. Not so attractive, is it? But we can all intimately relate.

> *"Most people don't realize that the mind constantly chatters. And yet, that chatter winds up being the force that drives us much of the day in terms of what we do, what we react to, and how we feel."*
> ~Jon Kabat-Zinn

Image Credit: This brilliant image is courtesy of Dirk Verschure, at Dirk's Big Bunny Blog.

You Are Not the Voice in Your Mind

One of the most important stepping stones in the realm of personal development in my life was when I fully realized that the voice in my mind was not really me. Catching on to the fact that the voice in my mind was little more than a succession of thoughts—with no correlation to me, my personality, or my true nature—was a real game changer.

When I'm worked up about something, it may come as no surprise that the voice in my mind spins on that one thing I'm angry about—over and over. The voice tells off the person or thing I'm angry with many times over. It yells, it shouts, it makes demands, and speaks its mind.

But the voice doesn't stop when I'm not angry. It's there all the time.

I used to follow my thoughts and look for meaning in them. But the vast majority of the time, my thoughts show up when I'm trying to sleep and say things like:
- *"I need to remember to call Tom tomorrow. Call Tom. Call Tom. Don't forget to call Tom."*
- *"Mike from yoga is kinda cute. I wonder if he's single."*
- *"I hope I didn't upset Laura when I went into her office with feedback earlier. Although . . . she is too sensitive."*
- *"Why are some people so sensitive?"*
- *"I should not have eaten that second cookie after lunch. I DEFINITELY have to work out tomorrow."*
- *"Maybe I'll try the new core class at the gym. I should look up the schedule now. No, I need to go to sleep now. I'll look first thing in the morning. I hope they have a class at 6:30."*
- *"I'm hungry. What kind of wine goes best with honey glazed salmon?"*
- *"I wonder if I'll ever get married."*

And when I'm going for a walk, I hear things like:
- *"I hope I'll make it to the coffee shop before it closes. I don't usually drink coffee after 2 p.m., but I am really dragging today. I hope it doesn't keep me up all night."*
- *"You're really forgetful. Always forgetting your jacket. It's chilly—I can't believe you forgot your jacket again. You could have at least tucked a sweater in your bag."*

- *"Awwww . . . what a cute dog. I think I'll get a dog. I wonder if my landlord would let me have a dog if it's under 40 pounds."*
- *"I should call my mom. Don't forget to call mom."*

These thoughts—and many more—would take place over the course of just minutes. How do these types of thoughts define me as an individual?

They don't.

So, I stopped spending so much time following the thoughts, trying to make sense of them, and analyzing why I had them—and started to detach from them. I simply became the one who listens to the thoughts, instead of the one who creates them.

If you're not yet convinced—try to take some time to listen objectively to your thoughts. Go ahead, evaluate them: Do they have meaning? Are they novel ideas? Do they hold valuable pieces of information? Will your thoughts change the course of your day . . . or your life?

From my experience, when you really tune in you'll find that the majority of what that voice "says" provides no value or meaning, and will have very little impact on your life. The fact is that life is going to unfold whether you overthink decisions or not, and the act of listening to those thoughts is generally a big waste of time.

And who has time to waste?

But don't take my word for it. If you're open to this concept, take a look for yourself with an open mind. As you observe your mind, ask yourself:

- Are my thoughts actually important?
- How relevant are my thoughts to the particular moment that I'm in?
- Are my thoughts about the past, the future, or the present moment?
- How pertinent are my thoughts to my current task or priority?
- How do those thoughts make me feel?

Michael Singer explained the irrelevance of the voice in our minds in a clear, concise, and beautiful way in the first chapter of his book, *The Untethered Soul*. I outline some of the key points in this chapter, but if you want to dive deeper into this concept and read about it in an elegant way, I recommend his book.

"If you spend your time hoping that it doesn't rain tomorrow, you are wasting your time. Your thoughts don't change the rain. You will someday come to see that there is no use for that incessant internal chatter, and there is no reason to constantly attempt to figure everything out. Eventually you will see that the real cause of problems is not life itself. It's the commotion the mind makes about life that really causes problems." ~ Excerpt From *"The Untethered Soul,"* by Michael A. Singer (Page 10).

Detaching From the Monkey Mind

When your mind is operating in monkey mind mode, you're not able to listen to what you really want in life—to what your heart is telling you. It's only when you're able to settle your mind and gain awareness that you can begin to align your mind with your heart and with the present moment. It's only then that you can begin to translate your visions into thoughts and actions. This is at the center of a mindfulness practice.

Life changes in positive ways when your thousands of thoughts are no longer ruling over your world. When you are truly aware of whatever it is you are doing—in the moment—it can defuse stress-producing thoughts and activity within the mind.

Meditation is what I've found to be the most powerful tool to develop the mind to be less of a monkey, and more like a calm and even-tempered deer. True, weird thoughts about my workout routine, my love life, and what I ate for lunch still arise—even during meditation—but I don't pay them much mind. Detaching from the endless chatter enables life to become less of a struggle and become more joyous, more simple, and have greater potential than we ever imagined.

The Power of the Present Moment

The problem is, our minds have a tendency to avoid the *right now*, and instead, they latch onto the past and the future. A study out of Yale University noted that the default mode network of our brain is where we operate from the most, which refers to our brain regions that are active during most of our waking hours when we're doing that thing that human beings do all the time—obsessing about ourselves, thinking about the past, thinking about the future, and doing anything except being focused on what's happening right now.

Basically, we are conditioned to avoid the present moment.

The study clearly showed that when we're operating in the default mode network of the brain, we mind-wander unconsciously up to 50 percent of the time. This mind-wandering state is not a place where people have reported to feel happy. Nearly half of our time is spent mind-wandering, with two thirds of the wandering time spent on stressful or neutral thoughts, thus sending us to unhappy places. So, avoiding the mindless trap of the default mode network and **figuring out how to spend more time in the present moment benefits our overall happiness levels—the most important thing in life to most people.**

This highlights the strength and power of the present moment. Unfortunately, our modern culture promotes anything but the present moment. We are conditioned to multi-task and look back and forward. How do we change this conditioning?

Findings to the study at Yale showed that meditation is the key. Meditators are able to not only turn off the default mode network of their brain while they're meditating, but even when they're not meditating. In other words, meditators are setting a new default mode network for the brain. And what's that default mode? They're focused on what's happening right now.

The topics of present moment and mindfulness have become popular in conversations, articles, and on TV—with research to back it up—it's become easier to understand how beneficial staying in the present moment can be. But with a mind like a monkey and a schedule filled to the brim, it can seem daunting.

If you're still not convinced that it's worth the journey with meditation, chapter three will come in handy for you, where we'll dive into the 10 top benefits and more scientific research.

I'll repeat the definition of mindfulness that I gave at the beginning of this section: awareness of the present moment without judgment. It may take on different meaning after hearing about the role that the monkey mind plays in your life, and the power the present moment can offer.

"All negativity is caused by an accumulation of psychological time and denial of the present. Unease, anxiety, tension, stress, worry—all forms of fear—are caused by too much future, and not enough presence. Guilt, regret, resentment, grievances, sadness, bitterness, and all forms of non-forgiveness are caused by too much past, and not enough presence." ~Eckhart Tolle, "The Power of Now: A Guide to Spiritual Enlightenment"

Ten Common Myths and Misunderstandings About Meditation

Now that we have a little understanding of what meditation is and why we practice, let's take a look at what it is NOT. As I mentioned, when I first considered starting a meditation practice, I was more than a little intimidated by the preconceived notions I had about what meditation was, and what sort of prerequisites and personality I needed in order to start.

A lot of the misunderstandings I carried were actually preventing me from meditating and from believing it would help me. I simply didn't think I was "qualified." But hearing the consistent buzz of the benefits eventually won me over.

Many of my students have since come to me with the same misunderstandings and myths about meditation. So let's set the record straight—here are 10 of the most common myths about meditation that I've heard and have held. I'm hoping that with a clearer set of expectations, meditation will seem suitable—and totally doable—for you, too.

Myth #1: You Must Clear Your Mind

A lot of people think that meditating is all about clearing the mind, and to them, that is the very notion that might seem too difficult or daunting.

Truth: Clearing your mind does seem difficult and daunting . . . because the mind is nearly (if not completely) impossible to wipe clear. It is the human mind's nature to jump around like a monkey, linger on thoughts, get stuck in cycles, and simply . . . think. That's its whole job. And in meditation, you can expect your mind to wander and get lost in thought. The practice of meditation is to observe what happens in the mind in a non-judgmental way, and when you "catch" it wandering (notice I said "when" and not "if") to then bring it back to the present moment. Again and again and again and again.

Myth #2: Meditation Is Time-Consuming

I used to think that I didn't have enough time to meditate. That would be my favorite excuse before I began a consistent practice—if I didn't have at least 20 or 30 minutes, I didn't think it would be worth sitting at all.

Truth: You really only need a few minutes a day to begin to feel the benefits of a meditation practice. The truth is, no one has enough time to do all of the things they want to do in a day.

Actually, many people find they create more time in their day by meditating, because they are able to be more present, more productive and more efficient with tasks at hand. Peter Bregman, author and leadership consultant, wrote in the *Harvard Business Journal*, "Meditation makes you more productive. How? By increasing your capacity to resist distracting urges." He continued, "Our ability to resist an impulse determines our success in learning a new behavior or changing an old habit. It's probably the single most important skill for our growth and development. As it turns out, that's one of the things meditation teaches us. It's also one of the hardest to learn."

Start with five minutes a day and see for yourself.

Myth #3: You Have to Feel Relaxed in Order to Meditate

If I waited until I felt relaxed before I meditated every day, my practices would be few and far between.

Truth: Meditation is actually a very effective technique to alleviate feelings of stress and overwhelm. It's true that if you meditate regularly, you'll become more adept at coping with inevitable life stress, but you don't have to feel at ease in order to sit down and meditate. Hopefully you'll feel more relaxed when your meditation is over. So if you're in a turbulent state of mind, you likely have the most to gain from meditating.

Myth #4: You Have to Sit Cross-Legged on the Floor

There are a lot of images of the Buddha sitting cross-legged on the earth under a Bodhi tree, yogis sitting in full lotus pose, and gurus in India sitting on straw mats with their eyes closed. This can seem uninviting if sitting on the floor is uncomfortable or unappealing to you.

The first time I sat down to meditate, I didn't have a cushion, pillow, or any instructions. I plopped down on the floor, crossed my legs into the best lotus pose I could devise, and closed my eyes. After a couple of minutes, my mind did focus—but it fixated on how my entire left foot was numb, and how I wished I had a meditation cushion to sit on. This is not the type of focus we hope for in meditation.

Truth: There's absolutely no need to try to look like Buddha when you meditate. As long as you're comfortable—and your spine is reasonably straight—you're in the right position for your meditation. You may find that sitting in a chair or on a pillow, cushion or yoga mat works best—or you may find that sitting cross-legged on the floor *IS* the position you feel most comfortable in—but you can make that call once you try it out. The only real rule here is to be comfortable. Flip to chapter four for a variety of sitting options for meditation, complete with photos.

Myth #5: Meditation Takes Years of Hard Work to Get it Right

What is "right" anyway, when it comes to meditation? What constitutes a good meditation versus a bad one? I used to think that meditating should always be a totally blissful experience if you're doing it right, and that if negativity entered your meditation you must be doing something wrong.

At the beginning, my meditations seemed like a grueling trip to the DMV, where you stand in one slow line, just to be given a number to then wait in another line, and then another . . . You know that severe agitation you feel when you have important things to be doing, but instead, you are waiting in a mandatory, yet inefficient line that seemingly has no end? This was how my meditations felt at the beginning. From where I was in my practice—and all the chatter, worry, and chaos that took place in my mind during my meditations—I figured I was doing something massively wrong and I must need to work harder at it, like years or decades. It turns out that I was wrong about this one, too.

Truth: One of the important principles of meditation is to be non-judgmental of your thoughts and experiences. So really, there is no right or wrong way to meditate.

There is no meditation that can be labeled good and none that can be labeled bad. As a beginner, you may need to call your mind back to the present moment more often, and there's nothing wrong with that.

Just like many other things in life, mindfulness is a skill that takes some practice. Meditation is the practice, and the more hours of experience meditating you rack up, the more mindful you will become over time. With a consistent practice, the benefits will build and the practice will come easier, meaning you'll be able to get into the meditative state faster and you'll be less affected by distractions.

While giant life changes generally don't take place after a five-minute meditation, I noticed many subtle, positive changes in the first week or two of my meditation practice . . . like patience, perspective, tolerance, and creativity. Research studies at Harvard have shown that it only takes eight weeks of meditating daily to create measurable changes in the brain relating to stress and awareness levels.

Myth #6: Meditation Is a Religious Thing

When many people first think of meditation, they think of Buddhist monks and "Ommm-ing" yogis sitting cross-legged on the floor, chanting and meditating.

Truth: It's true that the practice of meditation has roots from several religions and spiritual practices, but the practice of meditation itself does not need to have a religious affiliation, and there's no need to hold any beliefs or values in order to meditate.

Maria Konnikova, author and PhD in psychology from Columbia, wrote in a *New York Times* article, "Though the concept originates in ancient Buddhist, Hindu and Chinese traditions, when it comes to experimental psychology, mindfulness is less about spirituality and more about concentration: the ability to quiet your mind, focus your attention on the present, and dismiss any distractions that come your way."

If you want to Om, chant in Sanskrit, and pray to any God of your choice, you can do that during meditation. But that's certainly not a requirement.

Myth #7: People Who Meditate Are Always Peaceful and Mindful

This one makes me laugh. I definitely had a few surprising moments when I first became curious about meditation and witnessed unmindful acts from people I thought of as hard-core meditators . . . even teachers of meditation!

Years ago, I stood next to one of my first meditation and yoga instructors, as she flipped out on the barista for taking too long for her green tea latte. Granted, the coffee gal was texting instead of fixing my teacher's drink, but surely there are better ways of communicating urgency than raising your voice and creating dramatic facial expressions and movements with your arms. My teacher felt bad about the incident after we left the coffee shop; she was having a particularly bad day. And meditators are not immune to bad days or freakouts.

When I started teaching, one of the first questions a student asked me was if there were ever times where my mindfulness escaped me. My answer? An enthusiastic "Of course! Every day . . . I'm human. Meditating will help you live more mindfully, but it won't take away your role as a human."

Truth: I've been meditating for years, have a daily practice, and teach meditation—and I'd like to bust this myth first-hand. I have plenty of mindless and unmindful moments that I'm not proud of, and my friends who meditate and teach share the same sentiment.

But I will say that since I've started meditating, the amount of mindlessness in my life has significantly decreased, and when I do something that I consider to be unmindful, I recognize it quicker, observe it, and try to be non-judgmental and forgiving with myself. The more I meditated, the less mindless I became in other parts of my life, too.

But yes, meditators are still human, still perfectly capable of making mistakes, doing stupid things, and experiencing unpeaceful thoughts and moments.

Myth #8: You Must Be into Yoga (or at Least Be a Hippie or Vegan)

Crystals, chanting, levitating, gurus, mythical gods and goddesses, and *Nag Champa* incense . . . these are the things that came to my mind when I first heard about meditation. And I can't say that made me more interested in trying it out.

I've had students ask me all sorts of questions, like, "Do I need to stand on my head to meditate?" and, "What kind of yoga clothes do I need to buy in order to start meditating?" and, "Do I need to change my entire diet? I'm not a vegan, can I still meditate?" One woman told me that she liked washing her hair too much to start meditating.

Truth: People from all walks of life and cultures meditate. It's only becoming more widespread as the science-backed benefits of meditation become more known to the mainstream public. Meditation is for yogis, vegans, and hippies, but it's also for doctors, CEOs, bartenders, elementary school teachers, lawyers, nurses, and pretty much anyone looking to release stress, calm the mind, boost creativity, and increase their self-awareness, patience, productivity, and compassion.

Myth #9: Meditation Is Easy

"Meditating is just doing nothing, so what's the point?" This was one reoccurring thought I had years ago. Over the years, I kept hearing about the benefits and what meditation could do for me. And when I first started meditating—an activity I thought would be easy—it was actually super challenging. I was surprised and felt like a failure—and us Type A's don't like to fail. So I gave up. As an overachiever, I liked being good at things, especially easy things. I'd restart my practice and quit many times over my first couple of years meditating. I wanted to stick with it, but I thought I wasn't good at it. I mean . . . I was just sitting there, so it should be easy! But it was far from easy for me at the beginning. And Type As don't like to take part in things they aren't good at . . .

Truth: Starting a meditation practice was one of the hardest things I've done. But it's also been one of the most valuable. I wish someone had told me at the beginning to expect a challenge—I may have been more patient and understanding with myself.

It's important to set the expectation up front that being in the now—at times—can be the hardest place to be. If you know in the beginning that a meditation practice is meant to be rewarding and valuable in your life—but not always easy—you'll also learn to be patient with yourself.

Don't get me wrong, meditation can certainly be easy and effortless, and some people find that meditating comes natural to them. But for others, like me, the ease of meditation takes time. It's important to know that difficulty is normal at the beginning and *it does get easier*.

Myth #10: Type As Can't Meditate

As I've mentioned, this was a resolute belief I had for many years. I thought that just like some bodies are built for marathon running and others are built for acrobatics, some personality types would be suitable for meditation and others not at all.

I've always had a driven, go-go-go, Type A personality. Slowing down was hard for me growing up, and back-to-back activities were common for me even as a kid. As I mentioned in the introduction, I skipped lunch every semester in high school, just so I could take an extra class. I'd eat lunch near my locker during those five-minute breaks between classes. After school, I would go straight to dance class, play practice or choir, and I often went to work after that. The college and corporate chapters of my life looked even more ambitious.

When meditation was recommended to me to help with anxiety and stress, I didn't think it was possible. And when I tried it more than 10 years ago for the first time, I thought I had proven myself right. I couldn't meditate, and I thought it was because I was Type A.

Truth: Anyone can meditate. Actually, Type As have a lot more to gain than anyone, since they often move too fast through life, typically take on more responsibilities, and put more pressure on themselves to succeed. It may be a little more difficult for Type As to start out, but if they have the right expectations and guidelines, believe it's possible, and find some patience with themselves at the beginning, the rewards can be incredibly valuable.

"Meditation takes you beyond the mind's noisy chatter into the pure awareness that is the source of all your happiness, inspiration, and love." ~Deepak Chopra

Chapter 1 Key Takeaways:

- **It's normal to have thoughts during meditation.** Don't think of meditation as a means of emptying your mind. All humans have thoughts, and thoughts are the most common experience during meditation.

- **Meditation does not have to be part of a spiritual practice.** Although there are some styles and cultures that practice meditation with prayer and intertwine with religious faith, meditation has grown far beyond religious borders.

- **Meditation is not just a way to relax and feel calm during the time when we're meditating.** Meditation is a tool that trains our brain to be less reactive and more present with all things that cross our path in life.

- **We are happier when we're present.** And you can rewire your brain to spend less time in the past and future, and more time in the present. How? You guessed it—with meditation.

- **It's a myth that Type As can't meditate.** Actually, they can. And they have more to gain from a mindfulness practice.

Chapter 2:
Oh, the Many Ways to Practice Mindfulness

"When we walk like (we are rushing), we print anxiety and sorrow on the earth. We have to walk in a way that we only print peace and serenity on the earth ... Be aware of the contact between your feet and the earth. Walk as if you are kissing the earth with your feet."
~Thích Nhat Hanh

Being mindful is a state of mind. Meditation is just a tool you can use to become more mindful. But you don't have to sit cross-legged, or even sit at all, to practice mindfulness. All you have to do to practice mindfulness is to, in some way, practice being aware of the present moment without judgment.

Let's discuss the many ways you can practice mindfulness in your life. This list starts with the different types of seated meditations out there and leads into other ways to practice mindfulness. And, remember, this is just a sample, know that you can practice doing anything with 100 percent of your mindful attention, to get in the mindfulness mode.

Eleven Seated Meditation Styles and Techniques Explained

The first thing most people think of when they hear about mindfulness is seated meditation—which is by far the most discussed and studied tool for mindfulness. But the point of seated meditation isn't just to spend 5, 15, or 30 minutes of your day settling down and practicing mindfulness. The point of formal practice is to be able to bring the feelings you cultivate during meditation—peace, calm, present moment awareness—with you as you move through your days, your relationships, your job and your community.

There are many different types of meditation techniques, from mantra to mindfulness to sensory . . . and the list goes on. One of the most frequently asked questions I get is about the differences between the many styles, techniques, and programs. So I put together this overview of some popular types of seated meditation.

This is by no means meant to be a comprehensive guide to the many different forms, subdivisions, lineages, and meditations that are out there; it's just an overview of some of the most popular. Some of the styles I'll discuss are more traditional, others are Western styles or meditation programs that were inspired from the more traditional teachings, some overlap, and all are beneficial practices.

Remember—there is no best form of meditation—the best style is the one you will actually practice with consistency. So try a few styles out and see what feels best for you.

Mindfulness Meditation

Mindfulness meditation is the umbrella term for the category of techniques used to create awareness and insight by practicing focused attention, observing, and accepting all that arises without judgment. Although the origins of mindfulness meditation come from Buddhist teachings—predominantly Vipassana meditation, but also incorporates philosophies and practices from other Buddhist traditions—the style and way it's taught is nonsectarian and appeals to people from many different religions and cultures. Its simple nature and open philosophy has made it the most popular meditation technique in the West.

- **Who should try mindfulness meditation?** It's a great practice for anyone getting started in meditation or wanting to dive deeper into their practice. It is especially suitable for beginners who don't have access to a teacher, as the instructions are simple and there are many free and accessible resources and guided meditations on the Internet.
- **Well-known mindfulness teachers**: Dr. Jon Kabat-Zinn, Tara Brach, Sharon Salzberg, Joseph Goldstein, Jack Kornfield, Pema Chodron.

Mindfulness Based Stress Reduction

Mindfulness Based Stress Reduction, or MBSR, is an eight-week program that integrates mindfulness meditation and yoga with Western medicine and science. Dr. Jon Kabat-Zinn developed the program in 1979, drawing from many years as a student of Buddhism and yoga. He integrated these teachings with his background in science and designed a meditation program (although he doesn't call it meditation) that supports Western medicine to help people manage their stress, anxiety, illnesses, and chronic pain. He made the program extremely accessible and attractive to all types of people, and helped the general public understand that you don't need to be a Buddhist to practice meditation. You can find MBSR courses offered at medical centers, universities, hospitals, and clinics around the world.

- **Who should try MBSR?** MBSR is great for anyone suffering from chronic pain, illness or anxiety; anyone curious about meditation, but skeptical about spirituality; people who like evidence and data to support activity; and rookie meditators who want a supportive community to start their practice.
- **Creator**: Dr. Jon Kabat-Zinn

Primordial Sound Meditation

Primordial Sound Meditation, or PSM for short, is a mantra-based meditation technique rooted in the Vedic tradition of India. Drs. Deepak Chopra and David Simon revived this ancient practice at the Chopra Center for Wellbeing, and created a mantra-based meditation program anyone can practice. In PSM, each individual is given a mantra based on the vibration the universe was creating at the time and location of their birth. The mantra is used as a tool to take your mind to a quieter place. During meditation, you silently repeat the mantra, which creates a vibration that helps you slip into a place below the noisy chatter of the mind, and into stillness and pure awareness.

- **Who should try PSM?** Spiritually-minded individuals; people looking for structure in their meditation practice; and those new to meditation and serious about incorporating it into their lives.
- **Well-known PSM teacher and co-creator of the program**: Dr. Deepak Chopra

Vipassana Meditation

Vipassana is often known as insight meditation, translated to mean "to see things as they really are." Also a traditional Buddhist meditation practice, Vipassana emphasizes awareness of the breath, tuning into the air passing in and out through the nose. Vipassana also teaches you to label thoughts and experiences as they arise, taking mental notes as you identify objects that grab your attention. Each time you identify a label in your mind, you are then encouraged to bring your awareness back to your primary object, being the breath. There are several different types of Vipassana meditation that have evolved from the traditional style over the years.

- **Who should try Vipassana?** Vipassana is excellent for beginners, for people looking to practice meditation in an entirely secular context or combined with another religion or belief system, and for those interested in trying a silent retreat.*
- **Well-known Vipassana teachers**: Sharon Salzberg, Joseph Goldstein, Jack Kornfield, Michael Stone, Tara Brach

Vipassana is known for its silent retreats, offered around the world as a way to dive deeper into meditation practice and the inner world.

Zen Meditation (Zazen)

Zazen means "seated meditation" in Japanese. Most people know the meditation practice as simply Zen meditation, a type of Buddhist meditation where you focus your awareness on your breath and observe thoughts and experiences as they pass through the mind and environment, letting them float by. This may sound remarkably similar to Vipassana meditation, and that's because it is similar. There are some differences that would seem far more apparent to experienced meditators than those just starting out. One main practical difference is that in Zen meditation the emphasis of the breath is at the belly, instead of the nose (as in Vipassana). Another big difference is that posture is much stricter in Zen meditation than in Vipassana, with stringent attention on a straight spine, tucked chin, and hands placed in a special position over the belly. In Zen, eyes are instructed to be open, with a downcast gaze, and in Vipassana, there are not strict rules for the eye gaze, and beginners are typically encouraged to keep them closed.

- **Who should try Zen?** Zen is great for those who already have some experience with meditation; those who can handle rigid rules for practice; and those open to practicing with a teacher.
- **Well-known Zen teachers**: Thich Nhat Hanh, Joan Halifax Roshi, Adyashanti

Transcendental Meditation

Transcendental meditation, or TM, is another mantra-based meditation technique. As with PSM, its origin is from Ancient India and each person is given a personal mantra used for its vibrational qualities to help settle the mind. Although the purpose of the meditation and the technique itself is similar to PSM, there are quite a few differences, including the mantras themselves and how they are selected, the instruction of meditation, and the recommended length of time to meditate.

- **Who should try Transcendental Meditation?** People looking for structure in their meditation practice, those new to meditation and serious about incorporating it into life, and those who are willing to spend money on their mantra.

- **Creator**: Maharishi Mahesh Yogi

Loving-Kindness Meditation

Loving-kindness meditation is also known as *Metta* meditation, meaning unconditional kindness and friendliness. This meditation style also originates from Buddhist teachings, mainly Tibetan Buddhism. In the growing field of compassion research, the loving-kindness meditation has been proven to be particularly helpful with boosting empathy, positivity, acceptance, and kindness toward oneself and others.

The traditional loving-kindness meditation always starts with sending loving kindness to oneself, then continues to send it in this order: to a friend or loved one, to someone who is neutral in your life, to a difficult person, and then out to the universe.

- **Who should try Loving-Kindness meditation?** Anyone with low self-esteem, high levels of self-criticism, and a desire to grow more empathetic with others.
- **Well-known instructors who teach Loving-Kindness meditation**: Sharon Saltzberg, Pema Chodron

Kundalini Meditation

In Kundalini meditation, the main idea is that through meditation, you awaken your untapped Kundalini energy, located at the base of the spine. When this energy is released, it travels up the spine and leads to an experience commonly known as Kundalini awakening, which ultimately leads to enlightenment. Kundalini meditations can include breathing techniques, mantras, mudras (hand placements), and chants to tap into the power of the unconscious mind and bring it forward to energize and awaken the conscious mind.

- **Who should try Kundalini meditation?** Open-minded individuals and those looking to dive deeper into their spirituality.
- **Well-known Kundalini teachers:** Gurmukh Kaur Khalsa, Harijiwan

Yoga Nidra

Yoga Nidra is the Sanskrit phrase for yogic sleep. As the name suggests, it's a restful, deeply relaxing practice, and it originated from the Tantra tradition in yoga. Yoga Nidra is done lying down or in a reclined, comfortable posture, and although this may look like a nap, you are fully conscious during the practice. If you're in a class, teachers will usually recommend props, like blankets and bolsters, so you can find as much comfort and ease in the body as possible.

The meditation itself involves a step-by-step process of visualization and guided instructions that lead you into a deep state of conscious relaxation.

- **Who should try Yoga Nidra?** Anyone. Yoga Nidra is great for releasing stress . . . and who doesn't experience stress? It's especially helpful for those who are stressed out but have trouble focusing on just one thing at a time (like mantra or breath-awareness meditations).
- **Well-known yogis who teach Yoga Nidra:** Many teachers who teach asana also offer Yoga Nidra, including Dharma Mittra and Rod Stryker.

Chakra Meditations

A chakra is an energetic center in the body. It is taught that we have seven of them, each located in a different area of the body and each associated with a different color, sound, and energetic purpose. From the practice of yoga, chakra meditations can be very powerful, especially when focusing on and connecting with one element in the physical or emotional body at a time. Many chakra meditations use sound, specific placement of hands, and visualization techniques to connect with the chakras and bring healing energy to an issue or emotion that needs attention.

- **Who should try chakra meditations?** Chakra meditations are a great compliment to those already practicing yoga, those looking to heal something in their physical or energetic bodies, and spiritually-minded individuals.

Tonglen Meditation

Tonglen meditation is a Tibetan Buddhist meditation that is meant to connect you with suffering in an effort to help you overcome it. In the West, we are often taught to avoid suffering, sometimes through seeking pleasure, which is the exact opposite of how Tonglen teaches you to manage suffering and challenge. In these meditations, you develop an attitude of openness toward suffering, let go of negativity, practice giving and receiving, and cultivate compassion and empathy through the breath, visualization, and intention—for ourselves and others. The practice can be done in any comfortable position, whether seated or reclined.

- **Who should try Tonglen meditation?** Anyone dealing with difficult people, stress, and/or negativity; those struggling with self-criticism and self-doubt; those who want to cultivate compassion and kindness toward themselves and others; those seeking spiritual growth.
- **Well-known leaders who teach Tonglen meditation**: Pema Chodron, His Holiness the Dalai Lama.

Now that you have a breakdown of the various types of seated meditation, you probably realize that styles like Vipassana, Zen and Transcendental Meditation won't feel right for everyone. Although I do think that there is a style of meditation that will work for every personality, seated meditation may not be the place for you to start your work with mindfulness. After all, meditation is just one tool to gain mindfulness.

Let's take a look at other ways to practice . . .

Nine Ways to Practice Mindfulness That Don't Involve Sitting Still

My descent into mindfulness did not start with seated meditation. Yoga was really the bridge for me. I was a total fitness fanatic, and I'd been a runner for years. I would take long jogs with the purpose of not only getting some exercise, but also to clear my mind. Because I was interested in being physically active, I could more easily "swallow" trying yoga than meditation, which was far too intimidating and uninteresting to me at the time.

Connecting with the physical body in a mindful way, through yoga, taught me to open and settle my mind and slowly introduced me to mindfulness. What I quickly realized is that you don't have to sit still, or even sit at all, to practice being mindful. You just have to focus your attention and settle into the present moment in a nonjudgmental way.

The concept of movement while practicing mindfulness really appeals to me. My Type A tendencies made it incredibly difficult for me to sit still when I first started out. Even slowing down was difficult for me. But the practice of mindfulness has the power to take us beyond our internal struggles, self-doubt, anxiety, and judgment to a place that supports creativity, inner peace, joy and balance. Who wouldn't want some of that?!

So let's take a look at the many ways you can practice mindfulness in your life that don't involve total stillness. Feel free to add activities to this list that get you in the zone.

Yoga

Awareness of the physical body is a great place to begin your journey with mindfulness. In yoga, we start with the body—allowing the body and breath to lead, and the mind to follow, since the mind is the difficult component to tame.

Many people find their way to meditation and mindfulness through yoga because it's easier to focus on the physical body first. For me, it was the door that introduced me to meditation, and it was a great entry point to the entire world of mindfulness.

Plus, it can be a great way to get some exercise, stretch your body, and break a sweat. *Namaste*.

Creative Mindfulness

Try a more creative anchor for your mindfulness practice. Painting, drawing, playing the piano, decorating a cake—you don't have to be talented to practice mindfulness while getting creative. You just have to tune the external world out and focus completely on the activity. Coloring books and journals are an easy place to start getting mindfully creative.

Active Movement and Exercise

Choose your own exercise here to anchor your mind. Run, hike, surf, play a sport—anything that gets you in the zone is a great activity to practice mindfulness. Surfers often note that everything else in the world disappears when they're riding a wave, runners catch the runner's high when they're pounding the pavement, those who practice tai chi do so with such grace and attention—any activity that puts you in that heightened state of awareness will do the trick.

All you need to bring is your focused attention—and your equipment, depending on the activity.

Mindful Driving

I'm not going to recommend that you head down the highway, kick it into high gear, and slip into meditation. That would be a really bad idea.

But you can practice being mindful while you drive. The act of driving can be incredibly stressful; practicing mindfulness is a way to cut the edge off the commute and arrive to your destination with more focused attention.

The idea with mindful driving is that you really have to tune in and focus on—driving. That's it. But it's not as easy or common as it might sound to pay complete attention while you're behind the wheel. How many times have you arrived at a destination, but didn't really remember the drive there? We get lost in thought, in music, in phone conversations (over blue tooth, I hope), and all of a sudden, we are there! Or we are lost . . . either way, we realize our mind was not present while we were driving.

Next time you head out on your morning commute or take off on a road trip, see if you can tune into all the details from behind the wheel. This type of mindfulness practice can not only lower your stress levels on the commute, but also help you become more focused and present when you've arrived at your destination.

Mindful Driving Practice

- Get in your car, but before you put your key to the ignition, sit for one full minute with your eyes closed. Tune into your breath and your internal space, noticing how you feel and setting the intention for a mindful car ride.
- Start your car, turn off your music, silence your phone, and ease into a state of complete attentiveness.
- Keep your focus on the road and observe the sounds you hear as you drive. Really *see* the people, the buildings, and the landscapes you pass . . . notice the wind on your face if your window is down, the temperature, the whole experience of driving. Even if you've taken that route 100 times before, I bet you'll notice something new when you set the intention to drive mindfully.
- Each time you notice that your attention has shifted away from driving to other thoughts or sensations, gently bring it back to the car, and continue to observe, listen, and feel as you drive.
- Become aware of any emotions or urges that surface as you drive—notice how you respond to that someone who cut you off, notice if you find yourself speeding up at a yellow light, notice if you want to reach for your phone at a stop sign.

- Try to remain in observation mode and resist any temptation to act. Just focus on the experience of driving.
- Notice if you are speeding, and ask yourself: "Why am I in a hurry?" It's always best to leave yourself a few extra minutes to get to your destination so you don't feel the need to speed. Slow down.
- When you arrive, turn your car off and take another minute of silence before dashing off into your day.

Mindful Listening

Listening and hearing are two different things altogether. By the book, hearing is defined as "the act of receiving sound or information by the ear." While listening is defined as "the act of paying attention to sound, hearing something with thoughtful attention, or paying attention to someone or something in order to hear and understand what is being said, sung, or played."

When you are really listening to someone, you are hearing him/her. But when you are hearing something or someone, you are not always listening. Book definitions aside, let's take a look at the experience of listening versus the experience of hearing . . .

Listening requires 100 percent focus on the person who is talking. It's being with them in what they are saying, and taking in their words and emotions through all of your senses. Listening is hearing with every part of you. Think of a time you were talking with a friend, spouse, or therapist about an important situation in your life, and when the conversation was over you felt lighter, loved, and cared for. This is likely because they were with you fully. True listening is not as easy as it sounds.

It's actually a lot of work. After all, it requires 100 percent of our attention, and we are trained to multi-task. Cooking dinner while helping the kids with homework. Watching TV while working out. Responding to emails while on the phone. It's tough to focus on just one thing at a time and life circumstances don't always encourage this. Often when we're in listening mode, we're also in to-do-list-mode, laundry mode, or getting ready for the next task. This doesn't mean we aren't hearing what's being said. It just means we aren't fully present.

When we're truly listening to someone, we are holding space so the person can express whatever thoughts and feelings they want to share. We are inviting that information into our space and holding it open for them to feel welcomed, comfortable, at peace, and in loving company.

For some people, this is natural and effortless. For others, it's a muscle that will need to be worked, practiced, and improved.

> ## Mindful Listening Practice
>
> Meditation is a practice that trains the mind to focus . . . and trains the mind, body and emotions to be still and present with whatever comes up. And it does require practice. Just like in sitting meditation, you sit with whatever comes up when you're listening to someone . . . consider this a practice, too. Be with whomever you're with—don't just receive the information—fully listen to them. Invite whatever they say to the conversation to encourage them to open up further. Try to feel what they're feeling—relate, and understand. This is the practice of true listening.
>
> Next time you find yourself in the role of the listener, practice mindful listening. Follow these five steps to tune into the person you are listening to and see how it feels.
> - **Focus on the person talking**. Try to tune out other distractions—turn off your cell phone ringer, email notifications and TV—in order to fully focus on the person you're talking to. Try to keep your mind focused on the person talking . . . just like in sitting meditation, when

you notice your mind wandering, bring it back to the conversation.

- **Be present.** Nothing is worse than having to ask someone to repeat themselves when you should have been listening. Be present completely, and tune out thoughts about the past, future or anything irrelevant to the conversation.
- **Welcome whatever comes up in the moment.** Whether you agree with what is being said or not, invite the thoughts and emotions the person you're with is expressing. Welcoming the other person's words does not mean you agree or validate, it just means you are being there for them to express themselves. This includes offering facial expressions and body language that are neutral and warm. Try not to react to what they're saying too much with your voice, body, or face. Just be with them in a loving, present, inviting way.
- **Hold your tongue.** If you are in the listener role, just be there. There will be time for you to share your thoughts, offer advice, and share stories. But for now, when they are talking and you are listening, just hold the space for them and save your commentary for later. This may require patience.
- **Learn.** Take it all in and try to truly understand. Learning will require all of the above steps. If you're not present and focused, you could miss

> something, or even misinterpret or misunderstand. You also risk that the person you're with will feel ignored or not heard. And you'll likely be asked for your opinion or invited to share your thoughts at some point . . . you'll be able to do this with much more care if you truly understand the message delivered to you.
>
> Plus, when you learn about someone, it brings you closer to them and builds a stronger connection. That's why we talk to one another in the first place—to connect. So why engage in conversation if we aren't truly connecting or listening to one another?

Mindful Kissing

Kissing mindfully is different than kissing with a motive. A mindful smooch can't have any other purpose other than to smooch. It can't be a peck to communicate goodbye as you're headed out the door and it can't be attached to any expectation of where it will go next.

If you want to bring mindfulness into a kiss, just dive in and explore the kiss with all of your senses tuned in and remove your awareness from anything else . . . except the experience of the kiss.

Chores

While not as fun as mindful kissing, doing chores is a great time to practice being mindful. This will work with just about anything, you can try doing laundry, sweeping, or doing dishes mindfully.

Simply slow down and tune into the entire experience of being with your chore. If you're doing dishes, feel the hot water on your hands, smell the soapy bubbles, notice the process of the dishes transitioning from cruddy to clean. If you're sweeping, discover the different spaces and spots to clear with curiosity.

Michael Stone, a Buddhist teacher and social activist, told a story on his podcast once where he referenced the advice he gave to a student who was a high school teacher. To connect with the high school students more, and start class with a relaxed feeling, Michael suggested that she sweep the floor before class, as her students were walking into the classroom. It didn't matter that the floor did not need to be swept, he told her to think as she swept, "I sweep the floor with attentiveness, and I sweep my mind." This indeed helped her to settle and connect before she taught her class.

Mindful Walking

Walking meditation and mindful walking are great ways to anchor your attention into your physical body and slow down your mind and movements. When we're walking with a goal, we often move too quickly. When we walk with the purpose of practicing mindfulness, it's a totally different experience. We slow down, and we observe the act of walking through our various senses instead of just going through the motions.

While physically very different from seated meditation, walking meditation can be just as beneficial, offering us increased relaxation, decreased stress, and a boost in concentration. It's also an energizing practice since it wakes up the body.

Mark your calendars for 10 or 20 minutes tomorrow to head outside for a mindful walk—make sure you have no other destination other than to stroll and get some fresh air.

Once you get comfortable with your walking meditation practice, you can begin to bring in elements throughout your day—while walking to work, grocery shopping, or anytime you find yourself moving on two feet.

Find detailed instructions for a walking meditation practice in chapter eight.

Cooking

Cooking can be an incredibly mindful activity, or it can be a messy, loveless endeavor. When you cook mindfully, you are hyper-focused on the details of the meal you're about to create, starting with where it came from, so you can feel more connected to the food you're eating. You also consider how it will affect your body.

When you chop, you move with awareness and focus. Cooking can be stressful if you allow distraction and that overwhelmed feeling into the kitchen. Or it can be an opportunity to be creative and present.

Really, you can practice mindfulness in almost anything you do. Just set the intention of being mindful, hone your attention to the activity . . . and voila! You're on your mindful way.

"Enjoy simple things with total intensity. Just a cup of tea can be a deep meditation." ~Bhagwan Shree Rajneesh

Chapter 2 Key Takeaways:

- **There are many different styles and techniques for seated meditation.** Each one appeals to different personality types and different moods, so try different techniques and see what suits you best.

- **You don't have to sit still to practice mindfulness.** You can practice doing anything with 100 percent of your attention to get yourself into the mindful mode, or "in the zone."

- **Meditation is just a tool** you can practice to become more mindful.

- **There is no one best form of meditation.** The best style is the one you will actually practice with consistency.

Chapter 3:
Ten Benefits of Meditation That'll Really Help Type As

"If you correct your mind, the rest of your life will fall into place."
~Lau Tzu

Once you learn more about what meditation actually is, the next big question many people have is, "Why should I try it?" You're reading this book because you have a full schedule and a busy life, so why spend your time in meditation?

In this chapter, we're going to take a look at some of the impressive work of top-notch researchers who are discovering that meditation is chock-full of positives.

Skeptics are even picking up the practice, as research is getting tougher and tougher to debate. I am one of the skeptics-turned-meditators. My favorite question used to be, "But . . . how do we really KNOW that meditation is good for us?" In the past several years, scientists have been spoon-feeding us statistics that make even the biggest skeptic stop to take a deep breath.

I'm going to review what I feel are the top 10 benefits of meditation. So this section isn't a scientific ranking of the top benefits of meditation, it just includes what I feel are the 10 greatest gifts meditation has brought me—a typical Type A—over the years.

#1: Meditation Improves Focus, Concentration and Productivity

We have at least fifty thousand thoughts every day. Ninety percent of them are the same thoughts as yesterday and the day before. As busy people, we have better things to do than spend our time with the same fifty thousand thoughts and worries—over and over.

When you practice focusing on one thing at a time in meditation, you become more adept at focusing on one thing at a time in all areas of your life. With practice, you're essentially re-wiring the mind to not pay attention to things that don't deserve your attention.

The image on page 23 is a great visual of the 50,000 thoughts we have every day. This sort of mental noise is totally normal, but not necessary!

#2: Meditation Improves the Quality of Sleep

When you don't get enough sleep, or the quality of your sleep is not restful, it takes a giant toll on your mind and body. It probably comes as no surprise that even short-term sleep deficiencies can negatively impact your health, mental and performance state, memory, and weight. Battling chronic sleep deprivation can cause a host of more serious health issues, including diabetes, hypertension, depression, and obesity.

Yet an estimated 50-70 million Americans have some type of sleep disorder. Why? Surveys done by the Center for Disease Control and the National Sleep Foundation noted that most people are too busy concentrating on thoughts to fall asleep. Another popular reason people don't get enough sleep? They are too busy, and sleep isn't the priority.

Studies have shown that meditation and mindfulness practices have resulted in improved sleep quality for those who reported trouble sleeping, without the side effects of medications often used to treat insomnia and other sleep disturbances. Improved sleep through mindfulness meditation also meant less depression and fatigue, and therefore a better quality of life during waking hours.

#3: Meditation Reduces Stress

Stress is incredibly destructive in many ways. It's the cause of many diseases and inflammation of all kinds. For the purpose of this book, I'm just focusing on the consequences of stress when life gets too busy at work.

Stress inhibits creativity and courage—two things very important in the workplace—and increases confusion and indecisiveness—not so helpful at work. As leaders, innovators, and Type A hard workers, the byproducts of stress will kill our ability to be productive and successful.

Stress causes health issues (which we'll touch on in the next benefit), resulting in lack of clarity. Who is clear and able to be the best employee, parent, friend, and leader when they're stressed out and don't feel well physically?

Stress also increases feelings of self-consciousness, self-doubt, and insecurity: all unhelpful things when we're trying to be efficient and play many different roles in life. Meditation lowers cortisol levels, the stress hormone, and has the power to reverse the byproducts of stress.

#4: Meditation Improves Health

I'm not going to get into all of the health benefits of meditation—that would be an entire book. But it's important to note that most illnesses are at least in part stress-induced **and since meditation is such a**

powerful antidote to stress, it helps prevent and cope with most illnesses.

One interesting tidbit though, is that meditation has been found to actually boost the immune system. A study with the University of Wisconsin, Madison research team, found that those who meditate are able to produce significantly more antibodies to the flu vaccine than those who do not meditate.

Research also found that after a mere eight weeks of consistent meditation, research participants were 76 percent less likely than the controlled group to miss work due to sickness.

#5: Meditation Changes the Brain

Research is becoming more available as the subject of meditation and mindfulness rises in the field of neuroscience. Sara Lazar, senior researcher at Harvard led a series of studies that looked at MRI scans of participants who introduced daily doses of meditation. What they found was that gray matter grew in key areas of the brain having to do with self-awareness, compassion, learning, memory, emotion regulation, sense of self, and perspective taking.

Even better? Gray matter shrunk in the area of the brain associated with stress.

Harvard neuroscientists have reported that brain structures change after only eight weeks of meditation practice, at an average of twenty-seven minutes each day.

#6: Meditation Increases Compassion for Yourself and Others

Compassion is a beautiful antidote for insecurity, and working with our inner struggles. When we're mindful, we're observing instead of judging. Self-judgment causes insecurity, while self-compassion is one way to overcome insecurity. And when we let go of insecurity, we build confidence.

For research on the scientific benefits of practicing compassion, check out the website at the Center for Compassion and Altruism Research and Education at Stanford University.

#7: Meditation Boosts Creativity

Creative and innovative ideas are often born in spaces between moments, not during actual activity itself. Meditation settles and calms the mind to then spur creativity.

When's the last time you had a creative idea or solution in the middle of a busy day filled with back-to-back meetings?

#8: Meditation Brings Clarity

If you find yourself indecisive about your next step in life, meditation will support you with a dose of clarity. Practicing meditation helps you settle your mind so you can tune into your intuition and purpose, and get clear on that grandiose vision for your life.

Many times us Type As put a lot of effort into trying to get answers: Searching for rationale or advice on which job to take, whether or not to move, whether to move forward in a relationship, and other big life decisions. But often it's just the opposite that will help us arrive at the next step in life. Getting quiet allows the clear answers to come to us, instead of forcing them into our lives.

#9: Meditation Helps You Stay Present

If you aren't able to be present, you won't be able to work effectively, connect with others, or get clear on what you actually want in your life.

Think back to that Yale study I referenced in chapter one about the default mode network of the brain. The research showed that the human mind is conditioned to spend the majority of its time in the past and future, when science says that the present moment is when we're happiest. The study at Yale showed that meditation is a valuable tool to transform the default mode network of the brain so you can spend more time in the present moment—not just during meditation, but during life activity outside of meditation, too.

#10: Meditation Improves Happiness as a Skill

Yes, it's true . . . happiness can be trained in the same way we practice sports, video games, or cooking. It doesn't mean that external circumstances aren't going to impact your happiness. It just means you're going to be able to navigate them with more ease.

In the Harvard study where researchers looked at grey matter in the brain, they noted that, "Although the practice of meditation is associated with a sense of peacefulness and physical relaxation, practitioners have long claimed that meditation also provides cognitive and psychological benefits that persist throughout the day." So, those feelings of calm, present-moment awareness, contentment, ease, and joy that you feel during meditation won't stop when your meditations are over.

Again, meditation is just one form of a mindfulness practice. There are many tools and exercises to practice mindfulness so you can enjoy these benefits. (Go back to chapter two for ideas to practice mindfulness that don't involve sitting still.)

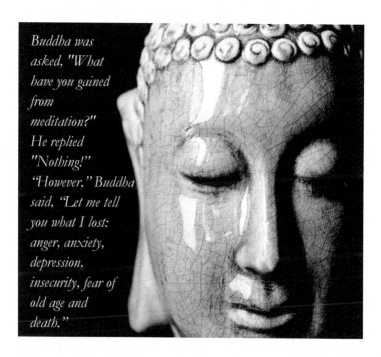

Buddha was asked, "What have you gained from meditation?" He replied "Nothing!" "However," Buddha said, "Let me tell you what I lost: anger, anxiety, depression, insecurity, fear of old age and death."

Chapter 3 Key Takeaways

- **Meditation helps you focus.** Humans have at least fifty thousand thoughts every day. Meditation trains the brain to focus on one thing at a time, improving the ability to focus and increasing productivity and clear thinking.

- **Meditation can improve your health.** Many studies have shown that meditation improves the immune system, quality and quantity of sleep, and decreases stress levels. And since most illnesses are at least in part stress-induced and meditation is such a powerful antidote to stress, it can help cope with—and may even prevent—most illnesses.

- **Meditation makes you happier:** Happiness is a skill that can be learned in the same way we practice sports, video games, or cooking. Meditation is the tool that strengthens the happiness muscle.

Chapter 4: How to Meditate—Steps to Get You Started

"Meditation should not be regarded as a learning process. It should be regarded as an experiencing process. You should not try to learn from meditation but try to feel it." ~ Chogyam Trungpa Rinpoche

Now that you know how meditation can help you, it's time to start practicing. When you're just starting out, meditating can be overwhelming, which seems like an ironic thing to say. After all, how can sitting still feel overwhelming? For me, sitting still was the hardest thing to fathom. This was partially because when I tried, it felt uncomfortable—mentally and physically. But mainly, it's because I never really learned *how* to meditate, and I had no idea where to start. The dozens of meditation styles and practices can make the basic steps sound far more complicated than they actually are.

If you're new, step back from all of the details and embrace these 10 rules. They'll guide the basic foundation for your meditations and answer the common questions many people have when just starting out.

Ten Rules for New Meditators

Rule #1: Be Comfortable

Sitting cross-legged in tight jeans, dress pants, or a short skirt doesn't make you want to stay put for very long. In meditation, you're aiming to focus your mind and remove distractions. But when you're too cold, overdressed, or sitting on rocky terrain, your comfort level can be more distracting than the punk band rehearsing next door. Wear lose-fitting clothing, sit on a pillow or cushion, and find a spot where the temperature is just right.

Rule #2: Be Alert

That's not to say that you need a shot of espresso before your meditations (I don't recommend that), but making sure you are rested enough so you won't fall asleep is important for your meditation to be effective. Your posture is important here, too. If you're sitting upright, you're more likely to remain attentive and alert. If sitting upright is not comfortable for you, refer to rule number one and choose any body position that allows you to be comfortable.

Rule #3: Start Small

When I first started meditating, I thought that if I couldn't sit for 30 minutes (or if I didn't have that kind of time to dedicate,) I might as well not meditate. Guess what happened? Not much for me in the meditation department. Since 30 minutes of meditation intimidated me, I opted out completely.

Once I gave myself permission to meditate for just five minutes, it propelled me into a steady practice. I naturally wanted to increase my time after that and soon reached my original 30-minute practice without it feeling like a chore. The key here is to find a schedule that works for you—however long or short it is—and get consistent. You can begin to enjoy the benefits with even a daily two-minute meditation.

Rule #4: Find a Quiet Space

You don't have to have a dedicated meditation space with Buddha paintings and prayer candles to meditate. All you need is a quiet corner of a room (or yard, or park…) where you can sit comfortably without distraction. And if you are met with noise or interruption, consider it an opportunity to further develop your willpower and concentration, inviting you to dive further into your meditation practice. If you can meditate in the midst of distraction, you're a pro.

Rule #5: Don't Try to Clear Your Mind

This is probably the most commonly misunderstood myth for meditation. The goal is not to clear your mind—that would be impossible, as the human mind naturally latches onto things. Calming, quieting, relaxing, and focusing the mind are all beautiful benefits that a meditation practice can bring. But wiping it clear completely? Good luck.

Rule #6: Turn Off Your Ringer

This really should be considered part of rule number four, but it's so important, and such a common mistake, that I'm turning it into its own rule. Before you slip into your meditation, turn your phone off, put it on airplane mode, or silence it (no vibrate mode!). There's nothing more distracting than hearing a buzz indicating you have a new email or text, which—even if your willpower is strong and you don't peek—will spin your mind into the cycle of wondering who it's from and what it's about. Our minds wander enough—you don't have to add to the monkey mind by inviting your smart phone to your meditations.

Rule #7: Be Consistent

It doesn't matter how small you start, the most important thing is that you practice. Ideally, at the same time every day so you create a habit. Consistency is more important than time spent—better to meditate every day for five minutes than once a week for an hour.

Rule #8: Be Patient

Don't expect to reach enlightenment after one meditation. One thing the practice teaches is patience, but you won't find that out unless you find some patience for yourself in the beginning. Release your expectations and get curious about where you're going instead of frustrated that you haven't reached some sort of unrealistic goal already.

Rule #9: Use a Timer

When I first started meditating, I would open my eyes to check how long it had been every few minutes, which was incredibly distracting. A timer solves this problem easily. Try the simple timer on your smart phone, or an app like insight timer. All you have to do is set it and trust that it will let you know when the meditation is over. If you're using your alarm, make sure to set it to a soft chime or gentle music so you don't get jolted out of your meditative state with a thunderbolt or an annoying "BRRRING."

Rule #10: Don't Judge

Go easy on yourself. It's tempting to judge your meditations by saying things like "my mind wandered too much" or "I only meditated for seven minutes today . . ." Once you're done, avoid self-sabotaging thoughts and simply celebrate. After all, you just sat still, which is actually an incredibly difficult thing to do in our society.

If you found your mind overactive and flitting from thought to thought, that doesn't mean you should scold yourself, it only means you're human. Thoughts will slow and gaps between thoughts will come with practice and consistency. So stop judging yourself for being human.

How to Sit for Meditation

There is another myth that you have to sit in full lotus pose or look like a human pretzel to meditate. The reality is that you can meditate in any position as long as you're comfortable. With that said, there are some important guidelines when you're finding a seat for meditation.

The first thing is simply to sit up straight—on the floor, on a cushion, or in a chair—it doesn't really matter where, but a straight spine will help you to stay alert for your meditations. You want to feel alive and energetic while you meditate—physically and mentally—and sitting in a physical position that is upright encourages that alert state of being.

Try it out so you can experience the difference. You'll likely find it's actually much easier to sit for longer periods of time when your spine is stacked properly, as opposed to slouching. When you're hunched over, not only will that promote a tired feeling, it's hard to maintain for longer stints of time and you can hurt yourself, causing pain in the back and neck as gravity pulls you down.

If sitting up straight is painful or uncomfortable in any way, lean against a wall or piece of furniture for support to encourage your vertebrae to be stacked. Remember, your number one rule for meditation is to be comfortable, so feel no shame for using props.

If your hips are tight or your knees feel achy when you sit on the floor, you have options. Sitting in a chair is a great place to start meditating, just find a chair that doesn't invite you to slouch. Notice if your favorite love seat encourages you to sink and make a choice that will better support your upright position. Over time, you may find that you become more flexible and may want to explore other positions.

Laying down is not the best option for meditation, but if you are in pain or there is some reason why you cannot sit comfortably, it's absolutely fine to lie down. There are some meditations that actually call for lying down, such as the body scan. But typically, this is not the position you'll use for your consistent practice.

Check out these eight variations for seated meditations, complete with photos where I demonstrate the ways to sit properly. The list starts with the easiest variation and gradually gets more difficult. Remember that everyone has a different body—you may find that crossing your legs for more than five minutes at a time makes your right shin fall asleep or your big toe go numb. You may find that one variation allows for a straighter spine. Try them all to find out what will work best for you.

Eight Ways to Sit for Meditation

In all of these variations, make sure your head is directly over your heart, and your heart is right over your hips, so your vertebrae are stacked. I recommend that you sit on the front edge of a rolled-up blanket, pillow, or cushion; this supports proper alignment—bringing the hips slightly above the knees and allowing the pelvis to tilt forward. Positioning in this way will emphasize the natural curvature in your lumbar spine, bringing stability to support a straight spine for extended periods. Plus, cushions also make your seat more comfortable, which is the number one rule.

In a Chair

Chairs make it easier for most people to sit still for longer periods of time, especially those with knee issues who have trouble in some of the floor-bound postures. If you choose to sit in a chair, make sure both feet are firmly on the floor. If your feet don't reach the floor, you can use a blanket or blocks under the feet, so they feel supported. You can either sit up straight toward the edge of your seat, or use the back of your chair for support if you need it. In either case, pay attention to the alignment of your spine, and note that it can be easier to sit up straight without using the back of your chair. A cushion or pillow under you may provide more comfort, and will bring your hips slightly over the knees so you're well stacked and supported.

Against a Wall

You can use the wall or a piece of sturdy furniture to help you sit up straight. Cross your legs or extend them out in front of you, whatever feels most comfortable. A cushion (zafu) or blanket under you works well here, too.

Kneeling with Support Between Knees

While you don't need to use a prop between your knees when you're kneeling, it takes the pressure off your knees and ankles, and is quite comfortable. You can use a pillow, a zafu cushion turned on its side, a rolled-up blanket, or a yoga block, and place it right between the knees and under your buttocks.

For the following cross-legged variations, I'll use references to "right foot" and "left foot," to make instructions easy to understand. Feel free to swap right and left in any cases to meet your optimal comfort level.

Easy Pose

Easy pose is a simple cross-legged position, where your knees are wide, your shins are crossed, and each foot is below the opposite knee. You probably loved this pose when you were a kid. I don't recommend easy pose for meditations over a few minutes; it isn't an incredibly stable seat and it can be easier to round the spine in this position. Plus, I've found that my feet tend to fall asleep faster in easy pose than any other meditation posture.

If you want to try it out for shorter meditations, it's great for stretching the knees and ankles, and opening the hips. Make sure to use a prop under you to elevate your hips.

Burmese Position

This is a variation of sitting cross-legged. If you're just starting out, use a meditation cushion or pillow. Sit on the front half of the cushion or pillow, bend your knees in front of you, and rotate your knees out to either side, sitting in a cross-legged position. Bring your left heel to the inside of your right thigh, and your right heel to lightly touch the top of your left foot, ankle, or calf, so it sits slightly in front of you. The sides of your knees may touch the ground and if they don't, you can use pillows or blankets under your knees for extra support.

Quarter Lotus Pose

Use a zafu or pillow here as well, and set yourself up in the same way as described for Burmese position: sitting on the front edge of your cushion, allowing your hips to open and legs to cross in front of you. Keep your left foot on the floor to the inside or below your right thigh, and your right foot to rest on the calf of the left leg.

Half Lotus Pose

Same position as quarter lotus, except you place your right foot to rest on the top of the left thigh instead of calf.

Full Lotus Pose

Full lotus is the most stable and symmetrical of meditation postures, but only if you're flexible and it feels comfortable for you. If you force yourself into full lotus, you can injure your knees. To come into full lotus, begin in the same way you set up for quarter or half lotus, but this time you'll bring your left foot to rest on your right thigh and your right foot to rest on your left thigh.

If you meditate in half or full lotus, make sure you're able to sit with a straight spine and with your knees close to the floor. If that isn't the case, take a modified meditation seat until you're open enough to maintain proper alignment in lotus. I also recommend alternating legs, from day to day or halfway through your meditations—so that the bottom foot spends some time on top—to create an even stretch and weight distribution.

How Long to Meditate

This is another question that can't be answered in the same way for everyone. Ask yourself this important question: *What is realistic?* What is a realistic amount of time I can dedicate every day to meditation?

The most important thing when you're first starting out is that you're consistent with your practice, so you should start with a time frame you think you can maintain. I can't stress enough to make sure that starting point is realistic.

When I first started out meditating, I thought I had to start out with a 20 or 30-minute window. I couldn't make it through the first meditation—even the first few minutes felt like eternity. It was like my monkey mind invited 32 of its friends to the conversation, escalating my worries and thoughts. I didn't make it through the second meditation either . . . or the third. By that time, I felt like I wouldn't be good at the whole meditating thing so I cut my losses.

I eventually tried setting a timer for just five minutes. I struggled through even the five minutes. I felt like I was cheating because my mind was spinning with thoughts and I would check the clock too early and often, but at least I made it to the end. From there, once I got comfortable with the five minutes of meditation, I slowly began increasing the time. This attempt was a much more organic evolution into meditation for me than starting out with a practice I was totally intimidated by.

Five minutes was a great place to start for my formal practice, but it may be different for you. I also started adding in what Janice Marturano, Founder and Executive Director of the Institute for Mindful Leadership and Former Vice President at General Mills Inc., calls "purposeful pauses." These are short (like one or two minutes) pauses throughout your day to remind yourself to be mindful.

It's notable to mention that over the years, I've had periods of time where life got full and though I had built up to a 30-minute practice, I would fall off the wagon because I didn't have the half hour. I wanted to be rigid and maintain the full 30 minutes of daily meditation, but found that when I was militant about my meditations, I sometimes would skip them entirely, thinking "If I can't do 30 minutes, I shouldn't do it at all . . ."

The most important thing to remember about how long you should meditate, is that **any amount of time is better than nothing**, no matter how new or experienced you are to meditation.

Chapter 4 Key Takeaways

- **Be comfortable.** The number one rule in meditation is to make sure you're comfortable. If you're not comfortable, you won't stick with it.

- **Start small and be consistent.** Create a meditation routine that you can stick with. Start small and work your way up. If you begin with an overwhelming practice, it won't last long.

- **Find the physical position that suits you best.** There are countless ways to sit for meditation. Explore the variations I provided in this chapter and find one where you're comfortable, stacked, and supported.

- **Adjust the length of meditation to work for your schedule.** The most important thing when you're first starting out is that you're consistent with your meditation practice; it's not how long you're meditating. So start with a time frame that's realistic. Any amount of time is better than nothing.

Chapter 5: How to Squeeze in a Meditation Anytime, Anywhere

"When people say to me, 'I don't have time to meditate.' I reply, 'Do you have time to feel like crap?'" ~Gabrielle Bernstein

You really want to meditate, but . . . you've got a lot going on. A full schedule. A demanding job. A busy life. How on earth will meditation fit into the picture?

We all have our excuses, and they're probably all valid because you have a busy life. We'll cover excuses and roadblocks more in chapter seven, but the biggest thing to note here is if you prioritize anything in life, you'll fit it in, no matter how busy you are. *If Oprah Winfrey finds 20 minutes twice a day to sit for her practice, you can spare a few minutes, too.* Meditation can be woven into your already busy life, if you decide it's a priority.

So if your schedule is packed with to-dos, but you really want to meditate, this chapter is for you. Remember to take these tips as foundation and adjust as you'd like. If I recommend fifteen minutes for a practice, but five is all you've got, go with that. Even one or two minutes of meditation each day could make a remarkable difference in your state of mind.

You may continue to think of other excuses, but there aren't any good ones when you're given permission to simplify and adjust meditation to fit in with your busy life.

When's the Best Time to Meditate?

The short answer to this common question is: Any time that works for you and your schedule. Just as I noted about the length of time to meditate, consistency is the key. So any time that you will actually be able to sit down to meditate consistently is the best time for you.

A Case for the Mornings

With that said, I love meditating as soon as I wake up. Nothing can get in the way of that meditation if I refrain from checking my phone, email, or getting involved with any other activity before sitting. I wake up a little earlier than I used to, I take care of bathroom business, and I meditate. It's that simple. You really have the best shot at following through with your meditations if it's before other activities begin.

Mornings are generally quiet compared to any other time of the day—it's the time before meetings, classes, responsibilities, and emails. It's helpful to match the quiet mode of meditation to the time of day that has similar energy.

The other great thing about meditating first thing is that I'm really not great at making decisions as soon as I wake up (I can't imagine anyone is), so with this routine, there's nothing to decide. What should I do this morning? The answer is always: Meditate. There's nothing else to remember or consider. When you're done with meditation, you can think about the rest of your day with a clearer mind space.

The first thing you do when you wake up will set the tone for your entire day. If you want to move through your day with ease, energy, awareness and confidence, start your day with activities that encourage those states of mind, like meditation.

Use those 10 minutes from the snooze button—or the first 5, 20, or 30 minutes of your day—to settle the mind and be still.

Advice for Non-Morning People
If you're not a morning person and want to transform into a creature of the a.m., consider this advice:
- Keep your blinds open to let the light in at sunrise. It's harder to get up when it's dark. This obviously doesn't work if your goal is to get up

before sunrise, in which case you can turn your light on as soon as your alarm sounds.

- Splash cold water on your face as soon as you wake if you find that refreshing and energizing.

- Splash hot water on your face when you wake if that feels good.

- Take a deep inhalation with peppermint oil under your nose to energize your senses.

- Hop in the shower first thing.

- Exercise before you do anything. Getting endorphins pumping is an effective way to charge your mind and body.

- Don't make giant changes overnight. It won't work if you are someone who hates waking up before 10:00 a.m., is used to going to bed after 2:00 a.m., and you try to shift your schedule four hours earlier overnight. Move your wake-up time slowly and implement morning rituals incrementally.

A Case for Evenings

A post-work meditation will help you ease the transition between work and home life. Meditating between work and home is great way to transition from one chapter of your day to the next. For many of us, we play very different roles at work and at home. Think of post-work meditation like a reset button to create some separation from your different roles in life.

If you're looking for greater work-life balance, taking time to consciously let go of whatever may have happened during the day and refocus your energy on family, friends, and evening projects or activities is a productive first step. Post-work meditation will help you take control of your personal time—and will generally benefit you and your loved ones tremendously.

How Can I Possibly Fit This Into My Crazy Evening Schedule?

The excuses may enter the picture again here, with full force. You might be thinking that you're usually running late to get the kids, make dinner for your spouse, go to yoga, or meet up with your friends for happy hour . . . how will this possibly work?

All you need is five minutes to get organized for the next workday and five minutes of quiet to let go of your busy day and de-stress.

Here's how: About five or ten minutes before you need to leave the office, wrap up your work and create a list of to-dos for the next day. Make any notes you don't want to forget about, problems that will need to be solved, and items that will be your high-priority to-dos the next time you return to work.

Then, you need to find the five minutes of quiet. Here are some possibilities of when and where you can squeeze in that post-work meditation:

Before You Leave Work
If you have a commute from work, meditating before you hop in the car or on the train will take the edge off of the commute. Once you get organized for the next day, turn off your computer, and sit quietly **at your desk** with your eyes closed so you can hit the inner reset button before you head home.

If you don't feel comfortable meditating at your desk, if it's too distracting for you, or if you just don't want to associate your meditation with work, try taking five minutes **in your car before you drive home**. Of course make sure this happens before you start your car.

On Your Commute
If you're not the one driving on the commute, try a short meditation **on the bus, train, or subway**.

If you are driving—and meditating at work or home don't sound appealing—**find a park or quiet space on your way home** to break up the commute, connect with nature, and let go of the worries from your day.

When You Get Home
If you find that your commute is particularly stress inducing—and some of the stress you are bringing home

is actually coming FROM your commute—you can take some time to meditate as soon as you get home from work.

If you know you can't find a quiet place inside, try a short meditation in your car outside your house. Park and turn your car off, then find a few minutes to sit quietly in meditation before walking into the house. This is especially helpful if you have young kids or social roommates.

If you can walk in the door and right away meditate somewhere that's quiet, waiting until you get home is a great option. But make sure you do it as soon as you walk in the door and before you do anything else. Your significant other, family, and roommates will support you—and thank you—when they realize that it will help you become more present with them.

It's important to highlight that after work is a far better time than later in the night to meditate. Some people find that their meditations energize, so practicing too close to bedtime may disrupt sleep patterns. Others find that if they meditate too close to bed, they will just fall asleep. The window between work and home is your best bet.

During Your Lunch Break

Lunchtime can be a great slot for your meditation. If your job is stressful, a mid-day meditation can help you release some of that stress and help you start your afternoons refreshed. Close the door to your office, find a quiet nook, or head outside and carve out a slice of your lunch hour to meditate. Stick with it every day for a month to make it a habit.

When You Feel Stress Surface

As soon as you notice stress begin to rise, or the feeling that you are running out of time, close your eyes and take a few deep breaths. Sometimes all you need to do is take a quiet moment to slow down your thoughts and settle your state, so you can focus on action items instead of the thoughts that you have too much to do.

Schedule It

Schedule your daily 10-minute mindful break. If you work in front of the computer, you can put it on your Outlook calendar or iCal so you'll be prompted. If you work at an office, tell your coworkers about it so they can support your silence.

There are also some useful smart phone apps out there that help schedule your meditations and keep you on track. Although it would be cool to have a meditation teacher that can fit in your pocket and whisper in your ear when it's time to sit still and breathe, an app is probably more feasible.

While our smart phones are often the culprits of distraction, they can also aid our mission to be mindful. The options are endless when it comes to meditation and mindfulness apps that offer keep-calm practices right from your device. And since reminding you to meditate is the most sought-out feature, they can come in handy if you find you're not being consistent with your meditations.

Check out these seven that offer, not only scheduling tools and reminders, but also different practices, sounds, styles, and other features.

- **Headspace**: This app calls itself a "gym membership for your mind." It'll give you 10 days of free, guided meditations so you can get a taste of the video and audio practices, as well as instruction for beginners on how to meditate. *Headspace* also allows you to track your progress so you can see how your meditations are going, and it'll send you mindful reminders to keep you on track. If you have 10 minutes a day, *Headspace* promises to train your mind so you can live a healthier, happier, more enjoyable life.

- **Buddhify2**: *Buddhify* presents excuse-free meditations. Since *Buddhify* comes with a variety of location and activity settings, you can find a practice to suit your mode, whether you're walking to work, trying to sleep, eating dinner, or feeling stressed out—it'll motivate you to keep on keeping calm.

- **The Mindfulness App**: This one leaves the shiny features behind and keeps it simple. The reminders are helpful in keeping you on-track and consistent, and the flexibility makes it work around your schedule, as guided meditations last anywhere from 3 to 30 minutes.

- **Simply Being**: This one is great for total rookies. A calming voice walks you through each meditation step by step, so your mind doesn't have room to get in the way. You can choose how long you want to meditate, and whether you listen to music or soothing nature sounds in the background.

- **Insight Timer**: This app features the soundtrack of Tibetan singing bowls and guided meditations by some of the best teachers in the world, including Jack Kornfield, Thich Nhat Hanh, and Eckhart Tolle. *Insight Timer* can be configured to play the bells at the start, end, and during pre-determined or random times throughout your meditation. It also offers a tracking tool, meditation journey, and global meditation community.

- **My Spirit Tools**: Meditations, mantras, prayers, breathing, and more. *My Spirit Tools* comes with over 20 practices you can mix and match.

- **Omvana**: Customize the meditations that work best for you. *Omvana* has the world's largest library of digital meditations, so you can mix and match sounds, music, voices, and quotes. *Omvana* also offers a recommendation engine, where they recommend practices based on your stress level and state of mind.

Chapter 5 Key Takeaways

- **Be consistent.** Creating a routine for your meditation practice is a good idea to keep you consistent.

- **There is no best time for meditation that works for everyone.** The best time for you to meditate is the time that works with your schedule and that you will actually do.

- **With that said, mindfulness is a lifestyle.** Mindfulness is not so much about your set meditation schedule, but more about a state of mind that the meditation schedule helps you create. The point of practicing meditation is to bring that present state of awareness into the rest of your life. Figuring out a set schedule for your practice is a necessary place to start. From there, the practice—and state of mind—will expand.

- **Not having time and being too busy are not viable excuses.** When you're given permission to simplify and adjust meditation to fit in with your busy life—and you make the decision that it's important enough to prioritize—you'll make the time and figure out how to integrate a practice into your life.

Chapter 6:
The Role of the Breath in Mindfulness

"Feelings come and go like clouds in a windy sky. Conscious breathing is my anchor."
~Thích Nhat Hanh

The mind and the breath are closely intertwined. Have you ever noticed that when the mind is unsettled, the breath gets shallow? And how when you take a deep breath, your mind slows down?

This is because they are partners in crime. When one moves, the other follows. When the breath expands, the mind expands. When the breath settles and slows, the mind settles and slows. When the breath constricts . . . you got it, the mind will constrict too. So it's almost impossible to talk about mindfulness and meditation without bringing the breath into the conversation—again and again and again.

By now you know that when the mind is left up to its own discretion, it'll do whatever it wants. We learned that in chapter one—the monkey mind naturally bounces from thought to thought. So we don't want to let the mind lead the breath. Instead, we encourage the breath to lead the mind. It gives you far more control over your mind when you allow the breath to be the anchor. After all, the breath is constant, it's always there and you can always count on it.

The average adult person takes an average of 12-20 breaths each minute, which is a fairly rapid pace. When we bring awareness to our breath—whether in yoga, meditation, or otherwise—the pace will be closer to 4-7 breaths per minute. In other words, when we are mindful of the breath and when we're relaxed, our breathing naturally becomes slower, deeper, steadier, and more nourishing.

Try This

The next time your mind is spinning or your emotions are high, take notice of your breath. Ask yourself:

- Has my breath sped up?
- Is my breath shallow?
- Is my breathing inconsistent?

If you are in a stressful situation or feeling emotional or nervous, it's likely that your breath is compromised and faster than normal. This is a sign of what's known as the fight-or-flight response—our body's primitive, automatic reaction that's intended to prepare the body to flee from a potential attack or threat. While the fight-or-flight response is not always a bad thing, when it's triggered, chemicals like adrenaline and cortisol are released into the body, causing a host of physiological changes, including dramatic shifts in our breathing.

Way back when, the fight-or-fight response used to protect us from the saber tooth tigers that might have snuck up on us when we were gathering berries. But in the modern world, there are few of us that face the threat of a saber tooth tiger, and the fight-or-flight response can cause far more harm than good. The problem is, it's triggered automatically by stresses both large and small.

There are ways of controlling the fight-or-flight response from wreaking havoc on your life, and the first step is to become aware of when it is triggered. Changes in the speed and quality of your breathing are one sign that fight-or-flight has been triggered.

When this happens, take that as a queue to slow it down. Follow these steps.

- Take three deep, cleansing breaths. Inhale through the nose, pause, at the top, then exhale slowly through the mouth.
- Then, take five deep breaths in and out through the *nose*. Stretch your inhale to a count of six, maintain the pause at the top, and stretch your exhale to a count of six. Move through this slowly and steadily five times.

That should take you about two minutes. When you're done, take a scan of your mind and emotions and see if you feel different. Notice if your nerves, emotions, or stress has settled in any way as your breath slowed down.

How the Breath Can Aid the Mind and Body

Oxygen is the most important element to us humans—far more important than even food and water. After all, we can go for days without water and some can go weeks without food. Humans can't go more than a few minutes without air.

What many people don't realize is that there are different ways you can breathe—and the way, style, and pace in which you breathe can have a dramatic impact on the state of your mind and body.

For example, most shallow breathing doesn't give our bodies enough oxygen to function properly. When your breath is consistently shallow, stagnant air, residue, and pollutants can accumulate in the lungs, which can lead to low energy, contracted breathing, and toxic buildup.

Deep breathing, on the other hand, gives our bodies nourishment and energy. Deep breathing not only supports healthier lungs, it ensures that oxygen moves through the blood and all cells, detoxifying, energizing, and nourishing along the way.

The average human uses only a small portion of their lung capacity because most people are shallow breathers. It isn't necessarily a problem to be a predominantly shallow breather, but problems arise when shallow breathing is the only kind of breathing you do.

So, it's important to pay attention to your breath and participate in activities that increase your lung capacity, and involve deep breathing, which can take many different forms. One of the reasons why exercising is so good for you is because it works the respiratory system. When you're working out and getting your heart rate up, your lungs and diaphragm expand as you breathe, making sure you're getting enough oxygen, releasing stagnancies and buildup, and making way for fresh air to enter into the bloodstream.

What's more? Aside from the host of health benefits we enjoy from increasing our lung capacity, participating in activities that encourage deep, expansive breathing also settles the mind.

Conscious Breathing and Meditation

Conscious breathing is one of the most powerful ways you can practice mindfulness. You've already learned about all of the ways you can practice being mindful in your life. For me, the breath has been the single most important part of my journey with mindfulness. Mindful breathing is the thing that shifted me from a person who *tried* to meditate regularly, to a person that *actually* meditated regularly.

I've mentioned this already, but it's important enough to repeat: Meditating was a struggle when I first began. Maybe many of you are reading this book because you've realized that meditation isn't easy for you, either. I spent years trying to love, or even just tolerate, meditation before actually embracing it. Since I was struggling with anxiety, when I sat in stillness, I felt the practice somehow highlighted my anxiety issues.

It wasn't until I began doing seated *Pranayama*, or breath work, every single morning right before my meditation, that my practice became consistent. To sit down and just start meditating is still super challenging for me. I need something else to settle my monkey mind first, something to help me focus. The thing that works for me is *Pranayama*.

There is a duality in each breath: It simultaneously grounds us and at the same time lifts us. Our inhales lift and expand, and our exhales ground and stabilize.

The word for breathing exercises in Sanskrit, and ancient Indian language, is *Pranayama*. If you break down the etymology of the word, you'll find both of these components create the actual word:

- *Prana*: Life force, which is an extension of the breath, symbolizing expansion.
- *Yama*: A restraint or discipline.

So the word pranayama includes the opposing forces of expansion and constriction. This for me has been an incredibly powerful way to start my meditations . . . and my days. Focused awareness—expanding and grounding with every breath—is a very physical way of anchoring your attention. Using physical cues is much easier to help you focus, than trying to root your attention on non-physical concepts.

The breath can have different effects on us, its role in mindfulness isn't just to settle the mind and prepare for meditation. There are different breathing exercises that impact the mind and body in different ways. Here are a few examples, followed by practices.

Try them and see for yourself how your physiology and state changes before and after the exercises.

Deep Cleansing Breaths

You're probably familiar with is a simple cleansing breath. If you've been doing the exercises along the way, you just did this simple exercise a few pages ago. I don't use this one sparingly. A deep, cleansing breath is always available to use when you need to hit the reset button.

Try It

- Take a slow, deep inhale through the nose.
- Briefly pause at the top.
- Then exhale slowly through the mouth with a sigh.

Do as many as you want, focusing on expanding fully with each inhale, and releasing fully with each exhale. Take your time with each breath—and the louder you are with your sigh, the better it feels. So don't be shy.

Alternate Nostril Breathing

This one is great for calming nerves and reversing stress. It balances our energy and syncs both sides of our bodies. It's based on the ideas that we have a left side, which is our lunar side, or our feminine side. And then we have a right side, which is our solar side, or our masculine or leadership side. Sometimes when they are out of alignment, we may feel scattered or uneasy. This breath practice is great for restoring that balance.

Whenever I feel a little frazzled, I move through a few rounds of alternate nostril breathing. This is also part of my pre-meditation breathing sequence—I move through a few rounds, then remain seated and shift directly into stillness. It helps to ground me before meditation.

For more about the benefits of alternate nostril breathing, and for steps on how to do this exercise, see practice #2 in chapter eight.

Breath Retention

Kumbhaka is the Sanskrit word for this powerful type of breathing exercise, where you focus your attention on the pause at the top of the inhale and/or at the bottom of the exhale.

Most people think of the breath as two parts: the inhalation and the exhalation. But there are actually four parts to the breath, including of course, the inhalation and exhalation, but also the space between the inhale and the exhale, and the space at the bottom of the exhale. Normally, this space is minimal and even unnoticeable. With a breath retention practice, you consciously extend the pauses at the top of the inhale and at the bottom of the exhale to create a holding pattern where you're ceasing to breathe in or out.

Breath retention is an incredibly effective tool to regulate mental chatter and improve concentration. When you are yearning for a new breath during a hold, you are devoting all concentration to this activity—training the mind to focus intensely on one thing at a time.

Plus, it feels amazing. It's like that feeling you get when you hold your breath for a while—like when you're swimming or in a porta potty avoiding a smell—and then you take another breath. Anytime you hold your breath at the top for some time, then release it; and anytime you hold your breath at the bottom, and then take a new breath, it gives you a surge of energy and a feeling of relief!

Try It

The pattern is simple: inhale, hold, exhale, hold, repeat.

- Exhale everything out through your mouth.
- Seal the lips and inhale slowly (on a count of five) through your nose until your lungs are completely full.
- Hold at the top for a count of five, keeping lips sealed.
- Exhale through the nose for five—taking all five counts to release the breath. Think of air slowly

being released from a balloon, that's the controlled pace of the release.
- When lungs are completely empty (you can release a little extra air at the bottom if there is still air left,) then hold for a count of five.
- Focus on creating space with every inhale and releasing with every exhale.
- Repeat.

*If a five-count seems easy, you can start increasing the counts as you breathe and hold.

> *"There is one way of breathing that is shameful and constricted. Then, there's another way: a breath of love that takes you all the way to infinity."* ~Rumi

Chapter 6 Key Takeaways

- **The mind and the breath are partners in crime.** When the breath expands, the mind expands. When the breath settles and slows, the mind settles and slows.

- **There are many different ways you can breathe**—and the way, style, and pace in which you breathe can have a dramatic impact on the state of your mind and body. For example, consistent shallow breathing can lead to low energy and toxic buildup, while deep breathing gives your body nourishment and energy.

- **Conscious breathing is one of the most powerful ways you can practice mindfulness.** Mindful breathing highlights the duality in each breath: how our inhales lift and expand us, and our exhales ground and stabilize us.

Chapter 7: Ten Common Obstacles for New Meditators and How to Overcome Them

*"If you really want to do something, you'll find a way.
If you don't, you'll find an excuse."*
~Jim Rohn

You may have read this book so far and said to yourself, "That's all great, but how do I actually DO all of these things in my life?" Maybe you've already found an obstacle or two in your way of meditation. Perhaps you've already tried meditation or other mindfulness practices, but have either given up or never *really* started.

By now you're aware of some of the benefits, since you've made it this far in this book. But, convincing people that there are benefits of meditation is the easy part. What most people struggle with is how to get going in a steady meditation practice.

If you've already decided that you want to try meditation and understand the potential benefits, but you are afraid you won't be able to succeed or follow through, this chapter is a must-read.

I became an expert in disappointing myself with an inconstant meditation practice. For years, I let meditation be the first thing to slip when life got busy, and I generally allowed life to get in the way. I came up with every excuse imaginable on why I had to put off my meditation "just five more minutes" or why "tomorrow will be a better time to meditate."

What I've found is that most of the time, the reasons why I wasn't meditating were the precise reasons why I SHOULD have been meditating. That's true for most of my students as well.

As much as we may want to practice and be mindful in our lives, the fast-paced nature of life can get in the way.

The bottom line is: Your mind will create excuses. You just need to have the tools to respond to those excuses. Armed with a host of reasons why your excuses to skip meditation are not valid and a clear action plan on how to overcome them, you'll succeed.

What follows are the 10 most common obstacles that got in my way, and how I moved past them to create a daily, consistent, valuable meditation practice.

Read through the roadblocks and identify which of them relate to your life. Ask yourself if the excuse is really true, or if it's your mind's creation. See if you can be open to some of the solutions before shutting them down, recognizing that the mind may want to create another excuse as to why you cannot overcome the roadblock. Do a cross-check to see if that's just the mind talking before deciding it's a valid excuse.

Time

By far and wide, my favorite excuse was that I didn't have enough time to meditate. I'm not alone on this, our culture fuels the busy badge, where people proudly proclaim that they're too busy to do the things they should and want to be doing.

But the truth is—and I heard this so many times before I listened—that once I began a consistent practice, time appeared. More time than I had before. Meditation retrains your brain to be more efficient, to focus, and to not spend time worrying about things that don't deserve your attention. Most people spend a lot of time repeating the same thoughts over and over in their mind. When we condition our minds to get clear and focus, we are able to get much more done.

The question remains: how do you find the time?

The answer is easy: Create it. I'm going to recommend specific times to guide you, but the best method is the one that works for you and the one you'll stick with.

Create Consistency

There is power in creating ritual. Studies say it takes 21 days or more to form a habit. So while it doesn't happen overnight, getting used to a new routine also isn't out of reach.

- **Choose a time and stick with it**: Choose a time, for example first thing in the morning, and stick with it for about a month. If that time slot doesn't feel right to you after the month is over, try a new time slot. But give the first try a fair chance; it will take some time before any change feels natural.

- **Try RPM**: I learned this acronym at the Chopra Center for Wellbeing, while taking my first Primordial Sound Meditation course. It stands for: Rise. Pee. Meditate. When you meditate first thing in the morning, nothing can get in the way of your meditation. Don't check your phone or email and don't start a conversation with your spouse or kids. Plan your wake-up time to be before life calls you to start the day, so you can get up and meditate.

- **Shorter and consistent beats longer and inconsistent**: Consistency is the number one obstacle people face and the single most effective guideline you can follow to help you avoid other obstacles.

Set Reminders

Schedule your meditations and mindfulness practice wherever you schedule your other important tasks and commitments, such as in Microsoft Outlook, Google Calendar, or on the white board beside your desk.

Whether it's a mid-day break for deep breathing, meditation, or a mindful walk, follow the tips in chapter five to help you set reminders and schedule your time to make sure you sneak your mindfulness practice into each day.

Use Technology

This may seem counter to the tip to limit technology, but this note is meant for you to use technology as a support to your meditation and mindfulness practices. There are many different apps out there that will help you stay on track and avoid skipping your practice. Revisit the seven meditation apps I recommended in chapter five to find the best one for your needs.

Start Small

Just start with one or two things at first and build from there. If you start with everything I'm recommending in this book at once, or choose an impractical length for your meditations, you'll get nowhere quickly.

So start with baby steps, and be realistic with yourself. As you build your practice from there, if the excuse of "not enough time" surfaces often, make sure to **remind yourself that any amount of meditation is better than not meditating.**

Limiting Beliefs

If you think meditation "isn't for you," or "is too difficult," try to get to the bottom of why you might believe those words.

As I mentioned at the beginning of this book, I didn't like the idea of meditation at all when I first heard about it, and I liked it even less when I first experienced it. My Type A personality made it difficult for me to slow down. **When I first started meditating, my mind would barge in, interrupt, and topple everything in sight;** it would ruin the experience for me. Agitation surfaced and uncomfortable, unfamiliar feelings would show up, in addition to the incessant mental chatter. I thought that was what happened to Type As who tried to meditate. I didn't realize that was just what happens to humans who aren't used to slowing down.

It took me a long time to understand that the phrase I used so much, "meditation isn't for Type As," wasn't actually true. It was just what I believed; just the story I was telling myself. And because that's what I believed, I proved it right.

Try to investigate for yourself why you don't think meditation is for you—if that is in fact what you believe. And then ask yourself, "Is it true?" and when you find your first answer, ask again, "Is it really true?"

Byron Katie, a world-renowned speaker and author in the realm of self-inquiry, always challenges us to dig deeper. In her four-step process called "The Work," Katie encourages people to ask themselves of any situation:

1. Is it true? (Yes or No. If no, move to number three.)
2. Can you absolutely know that it's true? (Yes or No)
3. How do you react and what happens, when you believe that thought?
4. Who would you be without the thought?

This exercise brings awareness to the truth behind our limiting thoughts. For example, 10 years ago when I held the limiting belief that Type As could not meditate, if I had gone through the four questions then, here is how the dialogue may have gone:

1. Is it true? *Yes, Type As cannot meditate!*
2. Can you absolutely know that it's true? *Well, no. Perhaps I have not given meditation a fair chance since I give up or get frustrated each time I try.*

3. How do you react and what happens, when you believe that thought? *I get frustrated that I'm a Type A and therefore cannot reap the rewards of meditation.*
4. Who would you be without the thought? *Maybe I would be a meditator!*

If you are telling yourself that meditation isn't for you, ask yourself the above four questions just to make sure and to gain some additional insight into what may be holding you back.

You Don't Know How

So many people don't get started in meditation for the simple reason that they don't know where to start. With mindfulness and meditation becoming more popular, resources and teachers are becoming more available.

Jump back to chapter three for a step-by-step guide for beginners on where to start.

Fear

Fear stops us from all sorts of things in life. It can show up in a valid way, stopping us from dangerous situations and people. But it can also get in the way of the good—relationships, life goals, fulfilling our dreams, changing bad habits, and picking up new ones that are good for us. Change can be scary.

If you sense fear might be your biggest obstacle, take a look at what might be behind it. Are you fearful of your own thoughts? Of failing at meditation? Are you scared of going deep and finding something in yourself that you don't want to find? Or are you just plain afraid of stillness?

I spent the first 25 years of my life full of anxiety and worry. Type As tend to worry more than most, and meditation was certainly a trigger of concern for me. I was fearful of not being able to calm my mind—which always proved to be true in those first minutes of meditation—and which caused my inner worrier to spiral deeper. I was also afraid of the quiet:

- *What would happen when my mind got quiet?*
- *What would happen if I could never find the quiet?*
- *What if each time I sat down to meditate, the space would fill with even more mental chatter?*

But, once I got the hang of it, meditation became the biggest thing that helped keep my worry and fear at bay. It helped me to settle and recondition my mind so it wouldn't head straight in the direction of worry every time something in life arose.

Asking myself these questions to put my fears into perspective has always helped, too:

- **What's the worst that could happen?**
- **What's the best that could happen?**

Place

Don't overthink this one or let it hold you back. For a location to meditate, it's best to find a quiet space free of distraction, where your pets, kids, spouse, neighbors, and cell phone won't interrupt you. But if that's not possible, anywhere works. If there's distraction where you are, it's just an opportunity to tune in even deeper to practice *not getting caught up in the distraction*. But it is more difficult.

Some people get caught up with the notion that they need a meditation room, an altar, and the perfect meditation chair to start a practice. And of course crystals, incense, plants, and a Buddha . . .

In reality, you don't need a chair, incense, or even a Buddha to meditate. All you need is you—complete with your thoughts, overwhelmed schedule, fears, and beginner's mind. A corner of a room works just fine to kick-start your practice.

Distractions

This one speaks not so much to distractions during meditation, but distractions in general. In order to be productive—and all of us busy bees want to be productive and efficient—you have to learn to work mindfully. This means focusing on one thing at a time.

Yes, there will always be distractions. Research says it takes 23 minutes to get back in the groove once you're distracted from the flow of thought. As a writer, it's a pet peeve when someone walks into my office and asks me if I have "just a minute." That minute derails my thinking because it's much more than a one-minute sacrifice.

Not to mention, we're already self-distracting all the time by checking our emails, texts, and notifications while mid-project or task, which can land us not only on a 20-minute journey into our Facebook feed, but also with the extra task of getting back on track.

Dr. Larry Rosen, expert researcher and writer in what he calls, "The Psychology of Technology," suggests an easy formula to combat the power our devices have over us. He came up with an easy acronym: ABC.

> A. Awareness. Know what distracts YOU.
> B. Breath. Calm and reset often.
> C. Choices. Make good choices for you.

I whole-heartedly agree that the first step is to build self-awareness. Know what distracts you and what helps you reset. Once you have a clear understanding of what steals your attention, you can find a practice that works for you to reduce those distractions. Which brings me to the next point...

Technology

Laptops, tablets, and smart phones are a big contributor to life distractions. We grab our smart phones when they beep or ring, and pretty much any time we're bored, curious, or in search of an answer to a question that seems urgent. This counters productivity if we're trying to get work done that requires real thinking; it can also disrupt moments of connecting with our family, friends, and real selves. Somehow, as a culture, we've developed extreme discomfort when we don't know the answer to something or feel like we are missing information. Rewind just a decade to the early 2000s and we didn't have the answer to every question at our fingertips; why can't we be comfortable not knowing something? Why must we interrupt ourselves to search for every small fact along the way?

I am someone who is very easily distracted, and I know I have trouble with willpower when I hear my phone ring or beep. So I have to get creative in setting boundaries to avoid feeling like technology has a hold on my life.

Below are five things that have worked for me to minimize distraction and stay focused.

Take a Technology Vacation
Designate device-free windows of time where you ditch your device and stay in the moment. Here are some ideas:

- Go for a walk every day without your phone.
- Ditch your phone every Sunday, making that conscious effort to take a technology break. If you like the idea but aren't ready to go that far, try Sundays from 12:00 p.m. to 4:00 p.m.
- Silence your phone every evening from 6:00 p.m. to 8:00 p.m. (or any other two-hour window of time).
- Take one weekend a month and go somewhere in nature without cell service. If you have more willpower, you can simply avoid using your device instead of going somewhere that doesn't allow you to connect. I don't have that kind of willpower, so I like to travel without service.
- Create conscious intentions around picking up your phone: ask yourself, "Do I really need that info or do I need something else?"

Turn Your Phone Off
This sounds easy, but it's not easy to follow through with. For many, our smart phone is our source of music, our

calculator, our watch, and our means of communication and entertainment. *Turn it off?! When it doesn't need a restart?!*

If that sounds impossible—or just plain stupid— try the next tip instead:

Put Your Phone on Airplane Mode

One of my favorite things about traveling is being disconnected. I get so much done on airplanes without the distraction of emails, Google, Facebook, and phone calls. It didn't occur to me until recently that I can just take the same approach when I need to crank out some critical thinking or writing.

If that still sounds impossible, start even smaller and try the next tip:

Silence Your Notifications

When you've got an important task at hand, turn off your notifications so you won't be interrupted. This means all app notifications that pop up on your screen: email, calendar reminders that ding or appear, and your phone's volume.

Set Up a Device-Free Zone

Designate one or two areas in your house where devices are not allowed . . . and stick to your rules. Once you're used to it, you'll find yourself enjoying those places most in your home. Good trial zones to begin with might be your bedroom, backyard, living room, kids' rooms, or kitchen table.

Once you begin to incorporate more technology breaks into your life, your instinct to grab your phone for every little thing will decrease; you'll rely less on technology, more on intuition, and find more mindful moments in your life.

Monkey Mind

A common excuse I would assert often was that "I was having too many thoughts!" I used that as fuel to resist my meditations.

What I learned over the years though, is that having too many thoughts isn't actually an obstacle—it's a reality. And it's the reason we practice meditation. The nature of our human mind is to have too many thoughts, and meditation helps us keep those thoughts under control. Flip back to the section, "The Monkey Mind Hard at Work" in Chapter one for a refresher on how much the monkey mind runs our lives.

One trick you can use when distracting thoughts are keeping you from meditating, is to think of the thoughts as though they were a boring story that provides no value and your breath as a fascinating tale. Each time you find your attention drifting away from your breath to thoughts—to the boring story—gently drift your attention back to your breath, always favoring your breath over distracting thoughts.

Lack of Self-Discipline

Trouble keeping yourself on track? You're not alone. This obstacle is the main reason beginners should set a consistent routine for meditation practice: so it becomes part of your every day, and you don't have to think about and agree to do it. It's just part of the day, without room for negotiation.

Once you create that habit, you'll notice the benefits, and they will be enough motivation to keep you on track.

Scroll back to chapter five to revisit those tips on setting up a consistent time for your meditations.

If you still find yourself lacking self-discipline, I recommend one of four things:

- **Find a meditation teacher or coach**: Some people swear by meditation teachers, insisting there is no other way to learn to meditate, while others say they are totally unnecessary. My belief is that everyone learns in different ways and has different needs. I do think that if self-discipline is an issue for you, meditation teachers can be a great way to learn the basics and get you on a regular routine. Many teachers will not just teach you the basics, but also recommend a schedule based on your life, and be there to support you and answer questions as you start your practice. Some will even regularly check in to make sure you "did your homework."

- **Find a meditation class**: Check out a local yoga studio or meditation center to see if there are any classes you can start attending. Even a once-a-week Tuesday night class will get you to a place where you'll feel called to meditate more regularly between classes. The Mindfulness Based Stress Reduction (MBSR) program is offered around the world at universities and health clinics. I took the eight-week program at University of California, San Diego Center for Mindfulness and loved it. Or, you can try an online version of the MBSR program.

- **Find a meditation group**: Try searching for a free meditation or Meetup group near you to meet like-minded people who get together to practice; groups can help keep you motivated. Another big benefit of practicing and learning in a group setting is that people will share issues they are having that you may not have experienced yet. By discussing those issues and learning about the solutions ahead of time, you're more prepared to deal with the same issues when you eventually encounter them in your own practice.

- **Find a meditation partner**: Even if your partner is as clueless about meditation as you are (or even more so), the purpose of a meditation partner is really to hold you accountable. If it's your spouse or roommate, see if you can find a time that works for you both and agree to motivate one another when discipline or enthusiasm on either side wanes. Sometimes just having someone to meet at a specific time is all you need to show up and practice.

Impatience

I remember getting frustrated with myself at first when I couldn't get it. This is another common trait of Type As, when the "I want results and I want them now!" mentality takes over.

It's important to realize, though, that it doesn't happen overnight. For us Type As, it might seem excruciatingly slow. You might want to give up at times. You will likely get impatient, like I did. Again and again . . .

. . . and again and again . . .

Just remember that there is no destination or goal, except to practice. Try one or two of these techniques and decide what works well for you. If you still don't see the benefits or like what the practice is doing for you after a few weeks, try a different technique.

This should be a rewarding practice, not a chore. You've got to find a practice that works for you, otherwise you won't stick with it.

One important expectation I'll set is this: It's hard. Sometimes being in the now is the hardest place to be. We all have times in our lives where we experience difficult situations and chaos in our lives and in our minds. Accepting those moments as they are is part of our mindfulness practice.

So try to muster up some patience. *Don't give up too fast.* Once you start to see the benefits of meditation—and it doesn't take as long as you think—you won't leave your practice behind. The beginning of a meditation practice is the hardest part; giving up prior to reaping the rewards is common. So before you declare, "It's not for me," give it a fair trial in a capacity that's feasible for you. Then watch what happens.

Chapter 7 Key Takeaways:

- **Your mind will create excuses to skip your meditations.** You just need to have the tools to respond to those excuses effectively.

- **Lack of time is the most common excuse to not meditate.** Once you begin a consistent practice, time will appear. Meditation retrains your brain to be more efficient, to focus, and to be more productive, which will create more time in your days.

- **Get to know what distracts you.** Once you have a clear understanding of what steals your attention, you can use that awareness to reduce those distractions.

- **Get to know what helps you reset.** Then, integrate those practices to help you recover from distraction and mind-wandering so you can be more productive at home and work.

- **You can always come up with an excuse as to why you can't meditate.** The next time your mind gives you an excuse—stop for a moment. Take a deep breath, and take a look to see if the excuse is actually valid. If it is, consciously make a decision to skip your meditation, recognizing the consequences. If not, take a seat—even if you only have a few minutes—and find some sense of stillness. Any amount of meditation is better than none.

"People say they can't meditate, what they really mean is that they won't make the time for it, or that when they try, they don't like what happens. It isn't what they are looking for or hoping for. It doesn't fulfill their expectations. So maybe they should try again, this time letting go of their expectations and just watching."
~Jon Kabat-Zinn, excerpt from "Wherever You Go, There You Are."

Chapter 8:
Ten Short Meditations and Mindfulness Exercises for When You're Way Too Busy

"Your mind already knows how to meditate. It is always resting on something—most often, however on thoughts based in hope or fear, the past or the future. When you begin to notice your thinking, you'll see that it is rarely focused on the present. Even if you try to stay in the present, you find that you keep slipping into some kind of worry or expectation or judgment. The mind is always commenting on something. In meditation, you practice consciously placing your attention on an object of your choosing instead of allowing it to gallop all over creation. It is not an easy practice necessarily, but it is a very simple one." ~Susan Piver, a Buddhist teacher and New York Times bestselling author. Excerpt from "The Wisdom of a Broken Heart."

Ready to practice? Good. This chapter offers 10 short meditations for when you don't have much time, but want to sneak in a practice.

In each of these exercises, you'll first find an introduction that explains when, why, and how the practice will be helpful. Simple steps for the exercise will follow.

You can also listen to the guided meditation I created just for readers of this book. **Download it for free here: http://mindfulminutes.com/Book-Guided-Meditation-Gift**

Practice #1: Five-Minute Meditation to Turn Down the Mind Chatter

Ever feel like you move through your day to the soundtrack of constant chatter? Like you're listening to a permanent radio stream of your least favorite station?

It's called mind chatter. Monkey mind. Inner gossip. And, as we now know, it's part of being human.

Everyone experiences the monkey mind to some degree, but for many of us, "noise" levels rise when stress levels rise, or when we're overbooked. The ironic thing is, the more mind chatter we experience, the less productive we're able to be. But the more we have on our plates, the more mind pollution we encounter. Which issue do you deal with first—quieting the mind chatter or clearing the calendar?

Once you're able to calm down the internal chatter, you'll notice that you're able to get more done, which leads to a quieter calendar.

This meditation will help you manage the monkey mind by working with that radio inside your head.

Simple Practice

- Close your eyes, settle into your seat, and take notice of where you are.
- Start just by noticing and observing what's going on in your body and your mind. Try not to judge anything you're experiencing . . . just observe.
- Now, bring your attention to your thoughts and notice what comes and goes. Continue being that silent observer of your mind.
- When the mind chatter arises (and it will), just listen for a moment, as if your mind were a radio. See if your thoughts have a certain flavor or mood. Try to detach yourself from them, as if they were just something you were listening to on the radio.
- Try to imagine those thoughts getting softer, bit by bit. As if someone was slowly turning down the volume of your thoughts. They are still there, but they are in the background.
- Stay with it for another minute or two, or five, as you begin to build a deeper, slower breath. When you notice the volume of your thoughts getting louder, slowly twist the knob to the left, turning down the radio of your mind and bringing focus back to the breath. Notice the back-and-forth as your mind chatter rises . . . then falls as you become aware and turn it down.

Practice #2: Breathing Exercise to Calm Nerves and Anxiety

Whether you're nervous about a presentation or interview, anxious about a conversation, or generally stressed out, this short breathing exercise will help you find your center.

Mindful breathing is a great tool to settle the mind and emotions. Specifically, alternate nostril breathing is the practice I find most helpful for calming my nerves and reversing stress.

When I'm feeling scattered and find myself doing too many things at once, or as soon as I sense panic or anxiety begin to rise, I move through a few rounds of alternate nostril breathing, or *Nadi Shodhana*. It's a great way to quickly restore balance and bring yourself into alignment, acting like a reset button for your mental state.

Simple Practice

1. Take a comfortable and tall seat, making sure your spine is straight and your heart is open.
2. Relax your left palm comfortably into your lap and bring your right hand just in front of your face.
3. With your right hand, bring your pointer finger and middle finger to rest between your

eyebrows, lightly using them as an anchor. The fingers we'll be actively using are the thumb and ring finger.
4. Close your eyes and take a deep breath in and out through your nose.
5. Close your right nostril with your right thumb. Inhale through the left nostril slowly and steadily.
6. Close the left nostril with your ring finger so both nostrils are held closed; retain your breath at the top of the inhale for a brief pause.
7. Open your right nostril and release the breath slowly through the right side; pause briefly at the bottom of the exhale.
8. Inhale through the right side slowly.
9. Hold both nostrils closed (with ring finger and thumb).
10. Open your left nostril and release breath slowly through the left side. Pause briefly at the bottom.
11. Repeat 5-10 cycles, allowing your mind to follow your inhales and exhales.

Steps 5-9 represent one complete cycle of alternate nostril breathing. If you're moving through the sequence slowly, one cycle should take you about 30-40 seconds. I recommend moving through 5-10 cycles when you're feeling stressed, anxious, or in need of a reset button.

Tip: Consistency is helpful, so try to match the length of your inhales, pauses, and exhales. For example, you can start to inhale for a count of five, hold for five, exhale for five, hold for five. You can slowly increase your count as you refine your practice.

Practice #3: The One-Minute Mindful Pause

Many people who are interested in meditation know it's good for them and why . . . that's why they're interested in beginning a practice. But sometimes that's not enough. Sometimes a 10-minute task—no matter how important it is—can feel overwhelming.

If you're one of those who think you don't have 10 minutes to meditate during your day, here's what I have to say: I bet you have one minute.

The assumption that meditation takes a certain amount of time, or setting an expectation around the amount of time you need to meditate, is something I generally disagree with. As far as meditation goes, to me, something is better than nothing, and for some people, it works better to ease in.

If you're overwhelmed with the idea of beginning a formal meditation practice—or if you need a plan B for finding mindfulness in your day when you skipped your normal meditation—check out this super short exercise.

Plan B

I'm still guilty of skipping my morning meditations from time to time. Because I know how much better I feel when I meditate, it doesn't happen often. But I am prone to getting caught up in the "too busy" mode.

By mid-morning each of those days, I noticed how much that morning stillness was missing from my day.

So I take a minute.

And then continue my day.

Then I take another minute. And another. And another. And it always helps me to sink more calmly into my day.

I'm not recommending that I, or anyone else, skip their morning meditation. But . . . if you do, there's a plan B. And it only involves a minute.

Just One Minute

Take one minute to yourself, 5 times a day, or 10, or 20. Plan it by how long your daily meditation usually is, or however long feels right to you. If you normally meditate for 20 minutes, plan to take one minute every half hour or so to make up for it. If five minutes seems right, take one minute five times during your day. That's it. I can relate when people say "I don't have 10 free minutes." But everyone has one.

When to take a minute? Here are some ideas:

- As soon as you wake up
- As soon as you get to work, but before you head into your day
- Between tasks, meetings, calls, or classes
- After you eat lunch
- As soon as you get home from work
- Any time you begin to feel stress rise inside of you
- Before a difficult conversation or undesirable task
- After a difficult conversation or undesirable task
- After dinner
- Before bedtime

The one-minute practice can complement your morning meditation, or replace it if you missed it or if the morning isn't working for you.

I recommend scheduling it so it becomes a habit and you don't forget. Try using an app to do the leg-work for you . . . just set them up and let the app tell you when to take a mindful minute. Sometimes it's good to customize the schedule and create one-minute windows ahead of time for consistency, while other times it works to let the app tell you when to take a minute. Try *Headspace* and *The Mindfulness App*.

Simple Practice

- Close your eyes.
- Focus on your breath, and slow it down: deep inhales and slow exhales.
- Repeat 6-8 times (or more if you have more than a minute!)
- Optional: Use a timer and set for one minute. Timers work well to make sure you don't get lost in meditation if you have something scheduled soon after.
- Enjoy a more peaceful state as you slip back into your day.

Practice #4: Meditation for Clarity—Attune to Your Heart

"Sometimes the heart knows things the mind could never explain."
~Ranjeet Singh

In many Eastern languages, the word for "mind" and "heart" is the same word: *Chitta* in Sanskrit, *Sem* in Tibetan, and *Citta* in Pali. When meditation moved to the West, we quickly associated it with the mind, which isn't necessarily a bad thing—meditation is a tool to train the mind. But we left the heart out of the practice, and the heart is at the center of a meditation practice, at the center of mindfulness and awareness. True meditation takes us to a place where we can be mindful of what's occurring in our hearts.

If you're looking for direction or clarity in life, considering a career move, looking for a new relationship, or considering a transition of any kind—try this practice. Even if you're not considering a change, try the practice—it's always healthy to be thinking about what positive changes you can make and dreams you can bring to life.

As you form your vision for a life change, a goal, or an intention of any kind, make sure you're tapping into not only your mind's energy, but also your heart's energy. The heart gives us a lot of valuable information . . . if we're able to settle our mind enough to tap into our heart and just listen. This can be difficult in our culture where we tend to overthink and over-plan.

As you consider life changes, take a brief, quiet moment to settle your mind, be silent, and align your mind with your heart. Follow this meditation to bring your mind and heart closer into alignment.

Simple Practice

Buddhists actually consider the heart to be located inside of the mind. Let's use that visual for our meditation:

- Sit up tall and close your eyes. Allow your body to be comfortable yet alert.
- Take a couple of cleansing breaths: inhaling slowly through your nose, exhaling through your mouth.
- Now begin your deep, slow breathing—in and out through your nose—maintaining a watchful eye on your breath.
- **Picture this**: Your heart is sitting at the center of your mind. It could be an anatomical heart, or a heart shape—it doesn't matter. Visualize this heart-mind resting as one unit at the center of your being.
- As you inhale, imagine your heart-mind expanding and glowing brighter, as if light is pouring in to fill the heart-mind with each inhale.

- As you exhale, imagine your heart-mind dimming and settling.
- With each inhale, watch it expand and glow.
- With each exhale, notice how it settles, relaxes, and dims.
- Stay with this visual for a few minutes—or as long as you'd like—and enjoy the relaxed and clear energy that follows.

Practice #5: Two-Minute Meditation to Focus

If you feel like you're mind is all over the place when you really need to concentrate, you're not alone. It feels like the act of concentrating is becoming more difficult by the moment. With beeps and dings interrupting your every move, it's hard to tackle tasks efficiently that require focused attention.

If you have a mountain of work to do or are sitting down to an important task and you're finding it difficult to concentrate, this two-minute meditation will help you to reset your mind and emotions in short order.

Simple Practice

- Take a comfortable, tall seat and close your eyes.
- Begin to bring all of your attention to your breath and slow it down.
- Inhale for a slow count of four, pause at the top, then exhale for a slow count of four, matching the length of your inhale with the length of your exhale.
- **Visualize your breath**: begin at the base of your spine and watch it rise up the length of your torso all the way to your collarbone, and then watch it release as it winds back down the spine.

- Notice the sensations of your belly and lungs as they fill up . . . and then release.
- Feel the cool air come in through your nostrils and warm air release as you breathe.
- When you feel the mind wander to your important task or to another place, just invite it back to focus on your breath.
- Allow your breath to lead and your mind to follow.

Practice #6: Pre-Presentation Practice—Meditation for Nervous Public Speakers

If you tell me that I'll be speaking or performing in front of a group of people—I'll be nervous. It doesn't matter how well I know the material, who the audience is, how much I meditate, or what kind of presentation or performance I might be giving. I've been this way my entire life.

The funny thing is, I've spent a lot of time in the spotlight. I spent 15 years in the theatre and dance world when I was younger, and I've been a singer-songwriter for the last decade, playing open mics and small gigs. I also teach yoga and meditation, where I find myself at the front of the room, and I regularly do presentations for clients and teams in my role as a content and marketing strategist.

After all this practice, you would think I'd be a wiz at public speaking, but I still struggle. The good news is, there are a few things I've figured out that help to settle my nerves before I take center stage. In no order of importance, here are some practices you might want to try—should you find yourself jittery before taking the spotlight.

Meditation for the Morning of Your Big Event

It should come as no surprise that meditating is an effective way to counter nerves. Simple deep breathing is all it usually takes to settle a nervous mind and a case of the jitters.

It's a good idea to put yourself in a relaxed mode for at least a few minutes each day leading up to your big event. On the morning of your performance or presentation, try this simple meditation for 10-15 minutes:

- Close your eyes and bring awareness to your breath. Slow inhales and deep exhales.
- Take a few minutes to practice breath retention: inhale for a count of five, hold for five, exhale for five, hold at the bottom for five. Take five to ten rounds.
- **Visualize the presentation or performance from start to finish.** Envision your arrival, your confidence as you enter the room, your engaging start to the presentation, your voice as loud and clear, and how your audience is engaged and interested in what you have to say. Visualize the entire process as smooth and successful.

Identify Your Fears

Ask yourself why you're nervous. Is it because of what people will think? Are you afraid you'll screw up? Have technology issues? Someone will ask a question you don't know the answer to? The audience will laugh you off stage or fall asleep?

Then remind yourself why you're doing what you're doing. It's probably because you are qualified, talented, inspiring, dynamic, or any combination or variation of them all. Use positive self-talk to remind yourself why you're presenting or performing in the first place. That should put your fears into perspective.

Worst-Case Scenario Exercise

What's the worst that can actually happen? Be realistic here, don't use the 0.00000000007 percent chance that there could be an earthquake mid-way through your solo, sending you sliding off stage.

Really and honestly—what's the worst thing that can happen? Get to know the worst-case scenario . . . I bet it isn't actually THAT bad.

Use Your Pre-Stage Anxiety

Depending on the dose of anxiety you're dealing with, you can use the adrenalin as fuel to power you through a high-energy speech or presentation in a more dynamic way. If you find the rush turning to nerves, take a few deep breaths and remember why you are doing what you're doing, or revert to steps one or two above.

Be Prepared

That doesn't mean memorize the speech or presentation word-for-word—unless, of course, you are in a play, then that's exactly what it means—but you should know your material thoroughly and be comfortable presenting it in front of a friend first.

Anticipate a few audience questions, or ask your friend what questions they have post-presentation so you can think through your response in the dry run. No matter how much you meditate or prepare, there will always be some stage fright—that's normal. But knowing your material builds confidence, and confidence is a powerful antidote to nerves.

Practice #7: Walking Meditation—Beat the Mid-Day Slump

Lunchtime can be a great time to practice mindfulness. It's around the time of day when there's the most sun, so a mindful walk can offer a bit of exercise, vitamin D, and a dose of the present moment. Moving your body is a great way to fight the mid-day slump and reset for the afternoon.

Why Try Walking Meditation?

We spend too much of our time rushing from point A to point B. Walking meditation is an opportunity to do just the opposite—think of walking meditation as a slow stroll without any other purpose or destination except to stroll—and be with any experiences that come up while putting one foot in front of the other.

Walking meditations can provide the same benefits as seated meditations—present moment awareness, relaxation, stress-reduction, focus—but in a different way. Walking meditation is also:

- **Energizing**: Walking is a great way to wake up the body and mind to get you ready for the afternoon. Walking during lunch or after work can be helpful to break the pattern of sitting in a desk all day. Walking first thing in the morning is

always an energizing, mindful way to start your day.
- **Convenient**: One great thing about walking meditations is that they can be integrated into your day, when you would normally be walking anyway . . . you can turn a simple and necessary walk from the parking garage to your office into a mindfulness practice.
- **Improves concentration**: It's no secret that it can be difficult to focus on one thing at a time in our fast-paced culture. Walking meditation encourages us to root our attention into our physical body, one step at a time. This can be an incredibly powerful practice in concentration and one-pointed attention.

As you practice during specific periods of time dedicated to walking meditation, you'll find that you'll begin to transform the steps you take during other times of the day, too. Walking meditation is a powerful way to transform something you do every day into a mindful, peaceful experience.

When to Practice

When you're first starting out, it's a good idea to set aside a window of time and specific location to practice walking meditation. **Lunchtime** is my favorite time of day for the practice, but here are some other times to consider:

- **Before sunrise**: The energy outside before daybreak is quiet and still. There aren't many interruptions and you are likely not expected to be anywhere else in life. If you're not an early bird, walking any time before work will energize you for the day ahead.
- **After work**: Release the day with a walk. Walking meditation can change your perspective and help you separate work from home life.
- **After dinner**: Any movement is helpful after a big meal, even if you're walking slowly. Set a peaceful tone for the remainder of the evening with a post-dinner mindful walk around the block.

How to Get Started With Walking Meditation

Walking meditations can be anywhere from 10 minutes to an hour. I recommend finding a walking path that is short—about 40 feet long—in a place without distraction or traffic (a park would be ideal). While you'll be walking much farther than 40 feet, the purpose of choosing a short, predetermined path, is that when you pace the same route back and forth, it requires almost no thought on where to go next and it minimizes the chances that you'll encounter something in your way. You get to know the route quickly, so you can focus on nothing but the experience of walking and let everything else go for the duration of your meditative walk.

Make sure you're wearing comfortable shoes, or even better—go barefoot—which will help you tune into your body and connect with the ground beneath you. Also, don't forget to leave your phone behind so you won't bring distractions into your practice.

While walking meditation can be practiced indoors, an outside route is almost always better, in my opinion. The combination of fresh air, sunshine, and peaceful movement is energizing and gets you closer to nature.

Simple Practice

- Start in mountain pose, with your feet hips-distance apart. Take a few deep, slow breaths. Begin to scan your body—starting at the feet and moving up the body—noticing any sensations in the body or mind before you begin to move. Notice the ground beneath you and your connection to the earth; notice any tension or stiffness as you scan and observe one body part at a time; notice any thoughts or emotions that you may be holding. Continue to bring awareness up the body piece by piece, all the way to the crown of your head.
- Start taking small, slow steps that align with your breath. As you inhale, step forward with your right foot, and exhale to place your left foot in front of the right. See how slow you can make your breathing and steps. Keep your pace

consistent, slow, and relaxed. As you walk, try to come to a rhythm, think "heel, arch, ball, toes," and repeat, placing one part of your foot on the earth at a time.

- When you arrive at the end of your path, simply stop, take a deep breath, and turn around to continue back the way you came.
- Make a conscious decision about where to gaze for your walk. Some people find it useful to keep their eyes focused down to avoid distraction, eye contact, or any external stimulants. Others like to take in every bit of the scenery—the sights, the colors, the sounds, the smells—noticing every detail while walking. Either way is fine and you might find that you switch up your approach depending on your location or mood, but make a conscious decision about which approach you'll take for each practice. If you are looking up and taking it all in through your senses, you'll be traveling the same route over and over again—so observe how much more you notice with each lap you take and as you settle more and more into your practice.
- Try to keep your attention on your breath and your steps. This is easier when your gaze is down, so you might want to start with that approach if you find your attention wandering. Just like in seated meditation, your mind will wander to other thoughts. Each time you notice your mind

wandering, just bring that attention back to your breath, your steps, and the present moment.

Remember, make sure you have no other destination other than to stroll, get some fresh air, and practice being mindful.

Practice #8: Post-Work Meditation to Let Go of the Busy Day

Do you ever take stress home from work with you? Have trouble letting go of your busy day? For most people, it's not easy to leave work stress at the workplace.

Stress is harmful enough when you have to bear it all day at work. And if you have a stressful or high-pressure job, the stress often doesn't stop when you head home. Work stress can carry into your commute, your personal relationships, your evening activities, and of course, your sleep. So when you bring it home, know that you're putting your own health, well-being, and happiness at risk.

So how do you leave the stress and emotions from your workday at work?

That's right, post-work meditations. We've already talked about the benefits of post-work meditations and how to squeeze them into your day, now all you need are the guidelines for a practice. De-stress, let go of your busy day, and ease into the evening with this meditation.

Simple Practice

- Sit up tall, get comfortable, and close your eyes.
- Take three cleansing breaths: inhaling slowly through your nose and exhaling audibly through your mouth.
- Now bring your left hand to your heart and right hand to your belly. Inhale through your nose in three parts—first to expand the belly, then the ribcage, then the chest. Hold at the top for a count of three, then open your mouth and let it out with a sigh. Repeat three to five times. You will feel your hands rise and fall as you breathe.
- Relax your hands into your lap, palms facing down, and inhale through the nose on a count of three, then exhale through the nose on a count of six . . . focusing on the exhale. Pause briefly at the bottom of your exhale before starting a new breath. There's no need to rush to the next breath, let it come to you. Continue breathing with this pace.
- With each long exhalation, focus on leaving something from your day behind to clear space for your evening. If there are specific thoughts or worries that are lingering, bring them to your attention and then on an exhale, imagine them sinking down into the chair or earth beneath you, leaving your body and leaving the space around you.

- Continue at a slow, steady pace for a few minutes, focusing on the exaggerated exhalation and sense of release that comes with every cycle.
- **Now imagine there is a giant door in front of you.** As you take a deep breath, you open the big door and notice it's heavy. You hold it open and as you exhale, you walk through the door and close it behind you. With this, you leave all of the stress from the day behind you—the conversations with your boss, complaints from coworkers, office gossip, pressure from deadlines, and difficult projects. All of the worries from the day remain behind the closed door as you continue walking forward and away from your workplace stress, allowing yourself to disconnect from the business of work for the time being.
- Finish your meditation with a few deep, cleansing breaths.

Practice #9: A Meditation You Can Do With Your Kids (but you can also do it alone)

Kids are amazing. I teach yoga and meditation at a hospital to kids undergoing treatment for cancer, and their families. One Saturday, I had a particularly interesting conversation with a five-year-old, and I think the story will help you understand the concept of this exercise.

I knocked on the hospital room door of a little boy I had taught a few times before who was recovering from a bone marrow transplant. Let's call him Noah. He was engrossed in a video game and hardly looked up when I peeked my head in. I knew he must have been really into the game because Noah loves yoga. His dad looked disappointed, he usually enjoys joining for the yoga sessions, too.

After a resolute "no," when I asked Noah if he wanted to take a break from his video game for some yoga, I looked at his dad.

"Well . . . if Noah doesn't want to do any yoga, why don't you and I just spend some time stretching?"

Noah looked up, curiously. But then looked back at his computer screen.

The goal is to convince the kids to participate in yoga. I consider half of my role as a yoga teacher at the hospital to be a salesperson for the program. I have to figure out how to make it appeal to the kids. They benefit so much from yoga and meditation, but a lot of times—for a million different reasons, video games included—they pass it up.

Noah's dad and I looked at each other, and with just a gaze, we made a silent pact to try to get Noah to join us for yoga. We began with some gentle stretches. Noah kept peeking at us, but every time we asked him if he wanted to join, he shook his head and pretended like he wasn't watching. So we started moving into some breath work and seated meditation without him.

I started talking about mindfulness and focus, and guiding Noah's dad through a simple mindfulness meditation. We were focusing on the breath leading the mind, when I opened my eyes to see if he appeared comfortable. He was fidgeting a little, and appeared to be working hard. With a full-time job and four kids—one of them in the middle of a four-month hospital visit—I imagine it's hard for him to slow down.

I turned my head and there was Noah, staring at us, smiling. "Noah, don't you want to join us?" I asked one more time.

"Ok!" he said enthusiastically. "But... um, I don't understand... my head is filled with all sorts of things. I can't help it."

"Well, let's give it try. What I'm telling your dad is to try to make your mind follow your breath."

"I still don't get it."

"Let's see . . . Noah, do you have a best friend? Someone you do everything with?" I asked.

He smiled again and told me his brother was his best friend.

"Ok, so you and your brother are best buddies. Usually when two friends hang out a lot, one of them is the one who decides things, the one who kind of leads. The other one is the friend that sort of follows the leader . . . do you think you are the leader or the follower?"

"My big brother is the leader," Noah said confidently, still full of smiles. His dad nodded and chimed in, "Noah will do anything Bryan tells him to do."

"Awesome," I said. "Ok so you and Bryan are inseparable. You do everything together. Let's pretend that your breath and your mind are best buddies, too, just like you and your brother. Let's pretend you are just like the mind—the follower—and your brother is just like the breath—the leader. Sound good?"

"Yeah! It's like follow the leader!" said Noah.

This time I was the one smiling. "Ok Noah, close your eyes and try to imagine you—remember you are the mind—following your brother. And remember your brother is your breath. Try to get your breath to lead the way, and your mind to follow it wherever it goes. So your brother—your breath—is calling all the shots."

"Take an inhale. Now take an exhale. Imagine your mind following your breath," I continued. "Inhale. Exhale."

I opened my eyes and saw a focused, smiley little boy, nodding his head.

"Oh, I get it now . . ." said Noah's dad. "I get it now," as he took another breath and dropped into his practice.

Simple Practice

Just as I explained to Noah and his dad, see if you can keep your mind following your breath through these steps:

- Close your eyes and sit up tall. Try to still your movements.

- Begin to bring all of your attention to your breath and slow it down. Allow your breath to lead and your mind to follow.
- **Count your breaths at the end of every exhale.** Don't let your mind count before the end of the exhale. This likely won't be easy or natural to you, the mind always wants to jump ahead, but coach it back. Allow it to remain focused on being the follower.
- Count to 10 or 20 or however long you want to dedicate.
- Every time the mind jumps ahead, bring it back to silently count the breath at the end of every exhale.
- Enjoy the state of presence that follows.

Practice #10: An Exercise for Stressful Times—Ultra Tense to Ultra Calm

It's a well-known fact that meditation is particularly helpful during times of stress. The problem is, that can also be when meditation is the most difficult. The long-term goal is to really formulate a consistent practice that helps you manage everyday stress so that it doesn't spiral out of control.

But life doesn't always follow the same plan you have, and we all have times in life where stress surpasses the amount that is considered normal or "everyday." These times are when meditation practices and relaxation techniques can come to the rescue. But these are also the times when your normal practice may have to shift; meditation may look different during ultra-stressful times.

I've learned this first-hand while struggling through various stressful situations. Even though I have a strong, daily meditation practice, I find it difficult to settle into my normal meditation routine when I'm carrying extra heavy weight on my mind and shoulders. And when my mind can't focus during meditation, it creates even more stress for me, which can end up in an unhealthy downward spiral. When I catch this and identify when I'm experiencing higher than normal stress levels, that's when I adjust my practice.

Here's one example: In 2014, I lost my job. This was a job I had for nearly eight years, and I was both surprised and devastated. I loved the people I worked with, the work I did, and I was extremely worried about my finances. I identified so closely with my career, spending well over 50 hours a week at that job for the better part of a decade. The layoff came as a total shock for many different reasons. When I got the news, I was able to be non-reactive and take time to fully process what was happening instead of reacting in the moment, as the pre-meditation me would have done.

However, in the weeks that followed, my normal meditations were particularly difficult. Feelings of uncertainty, betrayal, self-pity, rejection, and failure got in the way of my regular practice, and it became much more difficult to detach from the voice in my mind.

So I began experimenting with other styles. Sound healing meditations, body scans, visualizations, and other forms that encouraged my mind to go to specific and detailed places instead of just focusing on the breath or a mantra. These more "hands-on" meditations really helped my mind settle down when my stress levels and worries and doubts were through the roof.

Another example where I've learned this lesson is in coping with my mother's illnesses. She's been sick since I was eight years old, so I've learned to cope with her far-from-healthy state of being over the years. But when her illness flares up and she winds up in the hospital, it's extremely difficult for me to manage the stress. My family spent a lot of time in the hospital when I was younger since both of my parents were sick, so just being in that environment brings up difficult memories, uneasy feelings, concern, and anxiety.

Now, before I go to be with her when she's sick, I find it extremely helpful to ground myself through some simple exercises to alleviate some of the stress and pre-hospital anxiety. This also helps me to be more present with her when she's suffering.

The Negativity Bias

When we're extra stressed, our minds wander more easily than when we're not, and those thoughts of negativity and worry can become our obsession. This is just another glamorous part of being a human—our brains have a negativity bias, which means we are far more likely to focus on the negative things in our lives than on the positive. In fact, research has cited that our brains are about five times more likely to focus on a negative or stressful thought than on a positive one.

Rick Hanson, PhD, psychologist, and *NY Times* bestselling author said that, "the brain is like Velcro for negative experiences but Teflon for positive ones." Thoughts have a tendency to race straight to the darker places of worry and pain—and stay there—especially during tough times. This makes meditation more challenging than normal—since our brains have a hard time putting the stressful thoughts aside.

If you find your meditations more difficult when life gets super hard, try changing up your practice and creating stronger anchors for the mind—something more magnetic than the breath alone. Tough times are when you need meditation the most, and you won't stick with your practice if your mind refuses to take a break from worry.

Here's an exercise that includes detailed instructions to create that stronger anchor for your mind.

Simple Practice

This exercise for relieving stress is often referred to as the progressive muscle relaxation technique. Dr. Edmund Jacobson developed this technique in the 1920s, with the notion that tension in the body is usually found when we experience stress and anxiety in the mind. He created this technique to help people learn how to relax and alleviate tension when they are in a situation that makes it difficult for them to relax.

- Close your eyes and get comfortable. You can either sit in a comfortable position or lay down. Make sure your clothes are in no way constricting you and your shoes are off. Use any props, pillows, or blankets that may support your comfort level. Comfort is key.
- Take a few deep, cleansing breaths as you begin to still your movements.
- Bring all of your attention to your right foot, noticing how it feels. Then tense the entire right foot, making a fist with your foot, tense and squeeze it tightly. Hold this tension for a count of 10.
- Then release all tension in the right foot suddenly, relaxing it completely and observing the tension release and the foot feel lighter and more free.
- Take a deep, cleansing breath, then move on . . .
- Move your attention to your left foot. Same instructions for the left foot as for the right foot.
- Move slowly up and around the body, creating tension and contraction, immediately followed by the contrasting sensation of release and ease. **Follow each part with a deep, cleansing breath**. Here's a progression you can follow:
    - Right foot, left foot
    - Right ankle and calf, left ankle and calf
    - Right knee, left knee
    - Right thigh, left thigh
    - Hips
    - Butt

- Stomach and core
  - Chest and heart
  - Right arm, left arm
  - Right hand, left hand
  - Shoulders
  - Neck
  - Face
  - Whole body at once
- When you're done, spend at least a few minutes focusing on a slow, steady breath before slowly opening your eyes.

The body scan is another exercise that provides a more magnetic anchor during times of high stress. You can find a free, guided audio file of both the 45-minute body scan and the 20-minute body scan on this web page: https://health.ucsd.edu/specialties/mindfulness/programs/mbsr/Pages/audio.aspx

Chapter 8 Key Takeaways:

- **While finding a meditation teacher or attending a meditation class or group is always a great place to start**, following guided meditations or instructions is a great plan B when you want to sneak in a practice.

- **There are endless types and styles of meditation.** Try a meditation based on your mood.

- **Don't forget to listen to my free, guided meditation.** You can download it here: http://mindfulminutes.com/Book-Guided-Meditation-Gift.

"The real meditation practice is how we live our lives from moment to moment." ~Jon Kabat-Zinn

Final Note from the Author

"The present moment is filled with joy and happiness. If you are attentive, you will see it." ~ *Thích Nhat Hanh*

Thank you so much for sticking with me through this book and letting me guide you through the whats, whys, and hows in the world of mindfulness.

And, congratulations! Just by reading this book, you've taken a huge first step to finding balance and improving your life in a big way. The first step to building a consistent practice is often the hardest (as you now know, it was super tough for me.) But once you take it, there's no going back. Once you understand first-hand the powerful benefits that can come with a mindfulness practice—and the tools to get started—there's no reason NOT to integrate them into your life.

If you've already started a meditation or mindfulness practice and have found a steady routine with it: awesome. You're already a mindfulness rock star—stick with it. If you haven't yet started, there's no time like the present. Commit to carving out just five minutes to your practice each day for the next month, starting today. By the time a month passes, you'll be in the groove and won't need a reminder because you'll have seen for yourself how beneficial it can be for your overall well-being—which will be your motivation to continue.

And remember, not every time you sit down to meditate will be an enjoyable experience, especially at the beginning. That monkey mind of yours will run in circles; ***your job is just to practice guiding it toward stillness***. The more you practice, the easier—and more enjoyable—it becomes.

I began gradually increasing from my five-minute morning meditations after just a week. Bit by bit, my time increased and my mental chatter and anxiety decreased until I noticed that I simply didn't feel as awesome if I didn't do my practice. There are still days when I struggle with my meditations and my monkey mind takes over. Sometimes my timer goes off and I realize I may have just spent 30 minutes organizing a mental to-do list for my day. But at this point, those struggles are few and far between. And the cool thing is—no matter what happens during my meditation, I always arrive to my day with a more present feeling.

So now that you know what you have to do in order to find more balance and release stress in your life, what are you waiting for? Now that you know what you know—go ahead and practice it. You'll never regret taking the time for your meditations. (I don't think anyone ever has.)

Also, make sure you pay attention to subtle changes in your life once you start meditating. Notice things like:

- Calmer reactions to others
- More presence in your relationships
- Improved sleep
- Less stressful feelings
- More relaxed mind
- Enhanced ability to focus, concentrate, and problem solve
- Increased productivity
- Any comments that come from family, friends, and coworkers about changes they've noticed in you since you started meditating

Those subtle life improvements will stack up over time and be your fuel to maintain and/or grow your practice.

As a thank you for reading this book, please accept this gift from me: a free, guided audio meditation. This brief meditation focuses on settling stress and finding focus.

You can download the guided meditation here: http://mindfulminutes.com/Book-Guided-Meditation-Gift

Thank you again so much for reading and choosing me to help you as you start your journey with mindfulness. I would wish you good luck or some further words of motivation, but you don't need either. All you need is to take a seat and breathe for a few minutes: today, tomorrow, and the days after that, too. The motivation will come naturally as you realize the power of mindfulness in your own life.

If you have any questions as you start your practice, or want to share any thoughts on this book, don't hesitate to reach out. The best place to reach me is on my Mindful Minutes Facebook Page:
www.facebook.com/mindfulminutes
or on Twitter: @MelissaEisler. If you'd rather talk privately, or are interested in one-on-one mindfulness coaching, feel free to send me a note at Melissa@MindfulMinutes.com.

I'd love to support you in your journey towards healthy, balanced, and mindful living.

For more information, stories, meditations, and blogs about mindfulness, meditation and life balance in the modern world, visit www.MindfulMinutes.com.

Warmly,

Melissa Eisler

References

Barrett, B., M. S. Hayney, D. Muller, D. Rakel, A. Ward, C. N. Obasi, R. Brown, Z. Zhang, A. Zgierska, J. Gern, R. West, T. Ewers, S. Barlow, M. Gassman, and C. L. Coe. "Meditation or Exercise for Preventing Acute Respiratory Infection: A Randomized Controlled Trial." The Annals of Family Medicine, 2012, 337-46, accessed November 11, 2015, http://www.annfammed.org/content/10/4/337.full.pdf html/

Black DS, O'Reilly GA, Olmstead R, Breen EC, Irwin MR, "Mindfulness Meditation and Improvement in Sleep Quality and Daytime Impairment Among Older Adults With Sleep Disturbances." *JAMA Internal Medicine*, April 2015, http://archinte.jamanetwork.com/article.aspx?articleid=2110998

Bregman, Peter, "If You're Too Busy to Meditate, Read This." *Harvard Business Journal*, October 12, 2012, https://hbr.org/2012/10/if-youre-too-busy-to-meditate/

Brunette, Lisa, "Meditation Produces Positive Changes in the Brain." *University of Wisconsin News*, February 6, 2003, http://news.wisc.edu/8238

Carter, Christine, "Start Your Own Meditation Practice." *Christine Carter*, July 27, 2015, https://www.christinecarter.com/community/blog/2015/07/happiness-tip-take-a-meditation-break/

Cooper, Anderson, "Mindfulness." CBS News, December 14, 2014, http://www.cbsnews.com/news/mindfulness-anderson-cooper-60-minutes/

Epel, Elissa and Blackburn, Elizabeth, "Accelerated Telomere Shortening in Response to Life Stress." PNAS, September 28, 2004, http://www.pnas.org/content/101/49/17312.abstract/

Estroff Marano, Hara, "Our Brain's Negative Bias." *Psychology Today*, June 20, 2003, https://www.psychologytoday.com/articles/200306/our-brains-negative-bias/

"Guided Audio Files to Practice Mindfulness Based Stress Reduction." UC San Diego Health, accessed September 1, 2015, https://health.ucsd.edu/specialties/mindfulness/programs/mbsr/Pages/audio.aspx/

Hanson, Rick, "Confronting the Negativity Bias." *Rick Hanson*, October 26, 2010, https://www.rickhanson.net/how-your-brain-makes-you-easily-intimidated/

Hathaway, Bill, "Tuning out: How brains benefit from meditation." *YaleNews,* November 21, 2011, http://news.yale.edu/2011/11/21/tuning-out-how-brains-benefit-meditation/

"How Meditation Can Reshape Our Brains: Sara Lazar at TEDxCambridge 2011." YouTube video, 8:33, posted by "Tedx Talks," January 23, 2012, https://www.youtube.com/watch?v=m8rRzTtP7Tc/

"Insufficient Sleep Is a Public Health Problem." Centers for Disease Control and Prevention, accessed August 1, 2015, http://www.cdc.gov/features/dssleep/

Kabat-Zinn, Jon, *Wherever You Go, There You Are.* New York: Hachette Books, 2005.

Konnikova, Maria, PhD, "The Power of Concentration." *The New York Times,* December 15, 2012, http://www.nytimes.com/2012/12/16/opinion/sunday/the-power-of-concentration.html?pagewanted=all&_r=1

Marturano, Janice, "Simple, Daily Tips for Mindfulness at Work." Huffington Post, February 14, 2013, http://www.huffingtonpost.com/janice-l-marturano/simple-daily-tips-for-min_b_2686524.html/

McGreevey, Sue, "Eight weeks to a better brain." *Harvard Gazette,* January 21, 2011, http://news.harvard.edu/gazette/story/2011/01/eight-weeks-to-a-better-brain/

"Meditation: An Introduction." National Center for Complementary and Alternative Medicine, accessed September 2, 2015, https://nccih.nih.gov/sites/nccam.nih.gov/files/meditation.pdf/

"Mindfulness Journal Publications by Year, 1980-2014." American Mindfulness Research Association, accessed September 2, 2015, https://goamra.org/resources/

Pickert, Kate, "The Mindful Revolution." *Time,* January 23, 2014 http://time.com/1556/the-mindful-revolution/

Piver, Susan, *Wisdom of a Broken Heart.* New York: Atria Paperback, 2010.

Salzberg, Sharon, "Body Scan Meditation: Audio." *Sharon Salzberg,* February 13, 2015, http://www.sharonsalzberg.com/body-scan-meditation-audio/

Schulte, Brigid, "Harvard neuroscientist: Meditation not only reduces stress, here's how it changes your brain." *The Washington Post,* May 26, 2015, http://www.washingtonpost.com/news/inspired-life/wp/2015/05/26/harvard-neuroscientist-meditation-not-only-reduces-stress-it-literally-changes-your-brain/

Seppala, Emma, Dr., "Top 10 Scientific Benefits of Compassion." Stanford School of Medicine, The Center for Compassion and Altruism Research and Education, January 2, 2014, http://ccare.stanford.edu/uncategorized/top-10-scientific-benefits-of compassion/

Silverman, Rachel Emma, "Workplace Distractions: Here's Why You Won't Finish This Article." *The Wall Street Journal*, December 11, 2012, http://www.wsj.com/articles/SB10001424127887324339 204578173252223022388/

Singer, Michael, *The Untethered Soul*. Oakland: New Harbinger Publications, Inc., 2007.

Smalley, Susan, PhD, "Mind-wandering and mindfulness." *Psychology Today*, accessed September 2, 2015, https://www.psychologytoday.com/blog/look-around-and-look-within/201201/mind-wandering-and-mindfulness

Tolle, Eckhart, *The Power of Now: A Guide to Spiritual Enlightenment*. Novato: New World Library, 1999.

Verschure, Dirk, *Dirks Big Bunny Blog*, October 8, 2012, http://dirksbigbunnyblog.blogspot.com/2012/10/blog-post_8.html/

"Vital Signs (Body Temperature, Pulse Rate, Respiration Rate, Blood Pressure)." John Hopkins Medicine Health Library, accessed September, 2, 2015,
http://www.hopkinsmedicine.org/healthlibrary/conditions/cardiovascular_diseases/vital_signs_body_temperature_pulse_rate_respiration_rate_blood_pressure_85,P00866/

Apps and Online Classes, Tools, and Resources

Buddhify2
https://itunes.apple.com/us/app/buddhify-2/id687421118?mt=8

Dr. Larry Rosen
http://drlarryrosen.com

Headspace
https://www.headspace.com

Insight Timer
https://insighttimer.com

MBSR Online
http://www.umassmed.edu/cfm/stress-reduction/mbsr-online/

Meetup.com
http://www.meetup.com

My Spirit Tools
http://www.selfcultivate.com/my-spirit-tools/iphone-and-android/

Omvana
https://itunes.apple.com/us/app/omvana-meditate-sleep-focus/id595585396?mt=8

Simply Being
https://itunes.apple.com/us/app/simply-being-guided-meditation/id347418999?mt=8

The Center for Compassion and Altruism Research And Education
http://ccare.stanford.edu

The Mindfulness App
https://itunes.apple.com/us/app/the-mindfulness-app/id417071430?mt=8

About the Author

Melissa Eisler is a certified yoga instructor (E-RYT-200), certified Primordial Sound Meditation instructor, mindfulness writer and editor, and passionate about motivating people to live a healthy, balanced, purposeful life.

Originally from the East Coast, Melissa now lives in sunny San Diego, California, but appreciates her Type A nature and strong work ethic that developed before becoming a West Coaster. She's spent her whole life identifying closely with being busy, as someone who has always been enthusiastic about life and people and all of the opportunities that are constantly unfolding.

Melissa spent 10 years in corporate America working far beyond a full-time schedule; 5 at the stressful director level managing a large team. She now works as a senior content strategist and writer for the Chopra Center for Wellbeing, Deepak Chopra's mind-body wellness center, and freelances as a content strategist, writer and editor on the side.

Melissa teaches Vinyasa and Hatha classes at her favorite studio in San Diego, meditation and yoga to kids and families in the oncology ward at Rady's Children's Hospital, and yoga classes in corporate settings. She's also the creator of mindfulminutes.com, a personal blog about mindfulness and life balance in the modern world. Melissa understands what it's like to have a full calendar and serious career, and still find time for her meditation practice.

Her favorite part of teaching and writing about the world of mindfulness is the challenge of figuring out where people are in their journey, and meeting them there. It's about encouraging her students and readers to challenge their bodies and open their minds and hearts each time they step onto the yoga mat, sit down for a meditation, or open an article or book to read. It's about finding the right way to reach people and connect with them—so they can understand, relate to, and benefit from the practices of yoga and meditation.

Her hope is that by writing this book, she'll convince you of the possibilities and benefits of a consistent meditation practice, and inspire you to find some form of mindfulness that works for you.

CPSIA information can be obtained
at www.ICGtesting.com
Printed in the USA
LVOW01s0246210117
521734LV00006B/363/P